More Praise for *Relentless Sales*

"Powerful. At a time when the world needs more clarity on what is REAL, *Relentless* stands out as a reality marker of truth regarding the intersection of the human journey and sales performance. What makes this book special is that it goes way beyond just skill insights. It adds juice to the real tenets of performance: mindset, attitude and the ultimate secret weapon of faith. I challenge every sales person to read this book and begin to calibrate success."

Todd Zaugg, CEO of MATRIX (MX®) Achievement Sales Performance;
Author of *Warrior Sales Monk*

"I think I've read just about every sales book over the years and I have to say that *Relentless Sales* is a must read. The book covers a wide range of topics that most sales books miss. This is not another sales book that provides the reader a few good tips. This book helps you prepare holistically to excel in your job and in life! It's a must-read."

Heath Ritenour, Chairman & CEO, Insurance Office of America

"*Relentless Sales* is not just another book on improving sales; this book addresses issues to improve your life. Whether you are an industry veteran or just starting out, *Relentless Sales* is worth your time to read. But don't just read—absorb the truths and apply the principles that Jon lays out so clearly. Written from experience, *Relentless Sales* is an open and honest book—hard to come by these days."

Jim Henderson, President, Dynamic Sales Co., Inc.

"I've read dozens of business books and almost as many sales books, including the classics. *Relentless Sales* is a new classic! By far the most challenging task in building a business is curating and supporting an effective sales organization. This book rightly elevates the profession of sales, outlines well the blocking and tackling required for success and incorporates the rocket fuel of a biblical foundation for it all. I wish I had this book when I was growing our software technology company. It will be my top sales book recommendation going forward."

Richard Milam, Robotic Process Automation/AI Entrepreneur

"Jon has written a real winner here. His practical advice, real-life experience, and holistic approach to success—in sales and in life—give you real tracks to run on. Jon knows that while confidence is necessary, humility provides balance. He knows that in sales, the best 'win' is when everyone gets what they need. And he knows that in life, no man is an island. Finding your identity in something bigger than yourself is the key to happiness and success. No matter what profession you are in, being *Relentless Sales* will help you find fulfillment."

Brett Clemmer, President/CEO, Man in the Mirror, Inc.

"In this book, Jon shows the very essence of keeping God at the center of your life. Hebrews 11:1 says, 'Now faith is the substance of things hoped for, the evidence of things not seen.' After you read *Relentless Sales*, you will have an understanding of how to improve not only your sales, but also your faith. I can't wait to pass this book on to as many people as possible—I have total faith in its message."

Fitz Johnson, Esq., Public Service Commissioner,
U.S. Army Retired, and Entrepreneur

"Jon masterfully pulls us into his *Relentless* world and guides us on a path of what true success looks like not just in sales, but in life. He uniquely brings together business and faith in this book and it couldn't have come at a more needed time than right now. If true success is enjoying the presence of God in your life and then living that out in your personal and work life, then *Relentless* will provide the fuel to propel you into a new approach in how you achieve success."

Chuck Dunlop, Sales, MCC, US Army Veteran

"When writing, there's no such thing as a perfect book. However, Alwinson relied on the perfect source to guide his message. Faith is the foundation which influences every aspect of our lives (especially our profession). Alwinson's book is both timely and truthful. Read the book, apply the principles, and follow His guidance."

Paul Reilly, Author of *Selling Through Tough Times*

"I've had the pleasure of working with Jon the past 7 years and I've always admired his pure desire for development, his innate ability to lead others, and his relentless work ethic. These traits are also reflected in the teams he has managed. This book will give you the blueprint he has followed for many years."

Jamie Howell, Director of Sales, Boston Scientific

"Love this book! *Relentless Sales* should become required reading for everyone in sales. The sales process outlined and the questions and action steps at the end of every chapter are very helpful. Jon challenges his readers to live and work from a firm foundation rooted in Christ. Sprinkled with scripture, this book draws a strong correlation between our success in sales with our faith in God. Thank you, Jon, for a reminder about the amazing results that can occur when one blends their faith with their vocation!"

Kristi Lundell, MS, Medical Sales Professional, Honolulu, Hawaii

"A powerful reminder that sales is not just about techniques and strategies, but also about embodying qualities such as preparation, determination, and the faith to not give up, regardless of the obstacles that stand before you. Prepare to be inspired and equipped with the tools necessary to thrive as a sales professional ... and in life."

John Rivers, CEO, 4Rivers and 4R Restaurant Group

"As Jon's Pastor for over 10 years, I know his heart and inner man. Jon's ambition, infectious smile, confidence, and success all flow from a deeply committed inner man of faith. How I wish you could meet Jon. He is the real deal, and *Relentless Sales* truly reflects how God works in Jon and can work in you. While Jon gives great, practical sales advice, the gold of this book is the heart, faith, preparation, and inner strength necessary to be a great salesperson ... someone who is all about *Relentless Sales*."

Alan Scott, Lead Pastor, Lifebridge Community Church

RELENTLESS SALES

This publication is designed to provide accurate and authoritative information in regard to the subject matter covered. It is sold with the understanding that the publisher is not engaged in rendering legal, accounting, or other professional service. If legal advice or other expert assistance is required, the services of a competent professional person should be sought.

Library Of Congress Cataloging-In-Publication Data

Alwinson, Jon. Relentless sales: the skills, mentality, & faith needed to be great in sales / by Jon Alwinson; foreword by Pat Williams

p. cm.

ISBN 979-8-9892254-0-8. 1. Sales.

2. Faith. 3. Mentality. I. Title.

Edited by Zach Swee

Book Design by Keane Fine

Printing number

FP 23 24 25

7 6 5 4 3 2 1

THE SKILLS, MENTALITY, & FAITH
NEEDED TO BE GREAT IN SALES

RELENTLESS
SALES

JON ALWINSON

FOREWORD BY PAT WILLIAMS
Basketball Hall of Fame, Author, *Every Day is Game Day*

FORGE PRESS

A special thanks to our early review team:

Sandra Alwinson

Zach Swee

Pete Alwinson

Caron Alwinson

Scott McCurdy

John Riley

Jim Henderson

Justin Moses

Jamie Howell

Jeff Dew

Jim Gray

Mason Ailstock

Leslie Bishop

Alan Scott

Kristi Lundell

Stan Pietkiewicz

John Rivers

Brett Clemmer

Steve Brown

Fitz Johnson

Kanisha Parker

Stephen McClellan

Jonathan McClellan

Lindsey McCellen

Zach Bertilson

Ashley Bertilson

Joe Braun

Chuck Dunlop

Kristin Dunlop

Ryan Powers

Tyler Allen

Josh Keller

Brad Humphrey

Jacob Boyd

Mark Saso

Nate Roberson

Creston Liefried

Nick Panezich

Taylor Strickland

Justin Roberson

Kyle Mooney

Davis Anderson

Jessie Anderson

Caleb Neier

Brad Merrell

Caleb Hand

Eric Laing

Zach Steele

Daniel Lomax

Matt Ams

*"Your brand is your promise.
You have to deliver every day."*

CONTENTS

Acknowledgements

As a product of the public school system, I'll be the first to raise my hand and admit I received a great deal of support, guidance, and encouragement in the creation and development of this book. Thank you to my wife, Sandra, and our two kids, Ansley and Easton, for allowing me the time to write in the early and late hours of the day. To my entire family, I love you and appreciate your support. Thank you to my friend Joe who gave me the final encouragement I needed to start writing when he said, "Jon, you <u>ARE</u> writing a book. You need to just tell yourself you're going for it and commit to it." His encouraging words pushed me over the top to get going and make this book happen. To my friend and editor Zach Swee, thank you brother for everything along the way. You helped me polish this book into a very impactful tool for salespeople for generations to come. To all my friends across the country, including my work family (too many to name), I appreciate you and thank you for your support. You've influenced me more than I can say. My one request and "ask" from you is: if you find this book a valuable resource, will you share it with others? It would mean the world to me. Now, let's get started!

Foreword

Business, like sports, often comes down to one thing – winning. Right or wrong, we work in a Score Board Industry and a "what have you done for me lately" society. In order to be successful, you have to put forth maximum effort, invest in your development daily, have deep faith, and refuse to ever give up. This mentality is what allows winners to move to the top.

Sales is no different. It's a fast-paced, competitive environment, where everyone is looking for an edge or advantage. But that doesn't mean someone needs to compromise their values or take shortcuts on the path to success in sales. When done correctly, sales is one of the most noble and honorable professions of all. It's an industry built on the premise of seeking "mutual benefit," and the skills you develop in your sales journey can set you up for a lifetime of success. So the question becomes, how do you develop those skills?

In this area, sales and sports are very similar. Boiling it down, they each are a series of habits repeated over and over again, consistently over time. There are proven and 'sound fundamentals' (just like sports) that when properly followed and ingrained in you from daily discipline (plus a tireless work ethic) can help you become an elite performer.

That's why I love this book! The skillsets presented in *Relentless Sales*, combined with the mentality, faith, and holistic approach offered in this book, can help you build a foundation for an immensely successful career. I've had the privilege of cofounding the Orlando Magic, being General Manager for over 18 years, and working with the best athletes of all-time, including Charles Barkley, Shaquille O'Neil and others. I know what "good" looks like and I know that success demands a strong skill set and a relentless mentality. If your focus isn't on developing yourself in this way, you're going to be spinning your wheels as a sales professional.

That said, elite sales skills won't get you there alone. If that's all you have, you will wind up empty and unfulfilled. Identity, as Jon Alwinson so crucially lays out in Chapter 2, is not merely something that one does, it flows from who a person is. We truly achieve our potential once we allow God to build an identity that helps create strong relationships, rock solid moral and ethical integrity, and a commitment to help others along the way. This is a powerful insight into achieving *real* success, and it's one of many such insights I've found in the book you're about to read. No key-to-success topic is left out. I've enjoyed watching Jon's journey in his development, both as a man and as a sales professional, and I know you'll find a lot here to bring into your own career. As you read though this book, you'll find the playbook to success in sales, learn how to "shovel the rocks," get out there, and make it happen!

Go and master the skills to be Relentless in Sales and honor God throughout the process!

Pat Williams, Basketball Hall of Famer, Author, *Every Day is Game Day*

RELENTLESS

adjective

re·lent·less

: showing or promising no abatement of severity, intensity, strength, or pace: **UNRELENTING**

- Merriam-Webster

Relentless is a powerful word. It resonates deeply with me. In fact, I smile every time I see the word. For most people, life isn't easy. Yes, many of us come from loving families and were raised with good morals and ethics. Many of us were taught that God loves us and has a unique and special plan for our lives. But once you hit "the real world," life tends to get complicated, competitive, and difficult. What should I do with my life? How am I going to provide for a family? What industry should I get involved in? Am I working for the right organization?

For most of us who chose to enter the sales industry, we weren't born with a silver spoon in our mouths. Sales can be a very stressful and difficult industry. It requires a ton of energy, people skills, and *grit*. In my experience, families looking for an easy path for their kids typically encourage their children to enter industries other than traditional business-to-business sales, partially because the sales road is far too winding and difficult. Those who choose the path of sales usually enter for the opportunity to provide a better life and earning potential for themselves and their families.

There are some people in our business, however, who take the challenge of sales to **the next level** and rise above the crowd. These salespeople are committed to success. No amount of adversity, hardship, or resistance will stop them. They are obsessed with making something out of their lives and will stop at nothing to succeed. These individuals are not just hard workers. They are kind, generous, intelligent, loyal, and among the most dependable people you will ever meet. Their goal is to always do the right thing and to live their lives beyond reproach, with high character and with flawless morals and standards. These individuals are *Relentless Sales* people. They aren't necessarily born any different than you and I; they become relentless as they overcome adversity, develop discipline, and become deeply committed with conviction to do what's right.

Relentless Sales people are in high demand as every smart business leader wants to identify, hire, and incorporate these top performers into their organization. *Relentless Sales* people rise to the top and move the needle for their organizations. Furthermore, these people truly care about their customers. They know that when they put their customer first, truly listen, and work on solving others' problems, they become indispensable business partners whose customers enjoy their business relationship.

Relentless Sales people are not born—they are forged through adversity and instead of getting frustrated and quitting, difficult events only light a passion in them that pushes them toward greatness.

Finally, faith in God often plays a central role in their lives. In a world that puts everything ahead of God, *Relentless Sales* people are deeply rooted to a higher purpose in life. They are people of faith who care deeply for others and will still outwork anyone! Throughout this book we'll talk about how faith is a key differentiator in the world of sales. Maybe that doesn't perfectly resonate with you. If not, don't let it prevent you from learning the valuable skills and mentality needed for success that are taught in this book.

If any of what I've described of a *Relentless Sales* person intrigues you, then you've come to the right place. No matter where this book finds you—in a place of transition, curious about sales, inexperienced and looking to grow experience, a high achiever already accomplished in their field—I am confident you will learn how to deepen your ability to endure adversity, expand your sales skills, and fortify the mindset needed for success in sales. If this is you, welcome and let's get started!

INTRODUCTION

It wasn't supposed to be like this. Our business was supposed to become the next big entrepreneurial success story, but now it felt like that future was slipping through our hands. The sting of failure was starting to sink in as we sat at our local Panera Bread, drinking our customary hazelnut coffee that early Monday morning. Every Monday we'd meet to discuss our key business objectives for each week. Most of the time, these meetings were spent poring over our current sales numbers, brainstorming new opportunities, and planning our company's growth strategy while trading laughs about the latest conversation we'd had with a customer. But neither of us were laughing this morning. We had a good run, we gave it our best, but the unmistakable reality was clear: it was time to shut down the business we gave all our energy to build over the last 5+ years. We were beat down, emotionally drained, but certainly not defeated.

My older brother Joel and I created a business selling casual outdoor footwear including sandals, boat shoes, and apparel to outdoor retail stores throughout the United States. We had several innovative products, styles, and concepts, but we weren't able to protect any of them with patents or intellectual property rights. Eventually, we watched as larger companies copied and emulated the ideas we'd worked so hard to create and bring to market. Despite having some really cool products, our inability to protect our designs meant we were now competing with companies with deeper pockets, longstanding relationships with buyers, and massive market share. To add insult to injury, we made EVERY mistake in the book—something all too common for startup companies like ours. From overlapping job responsibilities to operational inefficiencies to hiring the wrong support team around us, we learned quite a few lessons—the hard way.

Joel was the CEO/visionary leader who helped raise the capital needed to fund our journey, and I was the inexperienced salesperson who was new to business and sales. I was tasked with selling to buyers who were significantly more advanced in their professional careers. They were seasoned, smart, and savvy. I was an energetic amateur in sales, and I was definitely out of my league from a business perspective. At the time, I was unaware how much I still needed to learn.

Although we had the best of intentions and gave it our all, our company didn't succeed as we envisioned. However, I can look back at the whole experience and smile (although sometimes *still* with a painful wince) because I recognize how going through that business experience developed a toughness and grit in me for which I am extremely grateful. These difficult lessons were paramount in kick-starting my journey to **studying and mastering the game of sales**. I promised myself I wouldn't fail again and that I would find a way to become both successful in life *and* highly proficient in sales. I embarked on a growth journey and for the last 15+ years, I've been fortunate to learn from some of the sharpest minds in sales and business. There have been ups and downs for sure. I've had the opportunity to win several decorated accolades both as an individual sales contributor and as a sales manager. I've also had my fair share of losses, mistakes, and failures. But through it all, I've remained committed to a lifelong study of sales. I've read every sales book I could get my hands on, intentionally sought out the best mentors, and most importantly, practiced daily the game of sales by *putting in the work*. Throughout this book, I will share some of the most powerful techniques, mindset advice, and tools other popular works on sales don't mention.

Whether you've been in sales for many years or are new to it, my goal in this book is to provide you with the valuable insights and lessons I've learned on this journey, giving you practical steps you can immediately implement to elevate your game today.

This book is different from most sales books. I've found that many of the typical lessons shared by the best sales leaders of the past and present leave out the most powerful key to being successful in sales. You see, there's a best-kept secret many sales leaders are either too scared to discuss or know nothing about. This secret frees you up to live authentically and lead courageously, and it actually makes you more attractive to your customers. The secret is trusting God and inviting Him to show you how to conduct your daily sales activity, relate better to customers, and change the way you see sales, business, and life.

As a follower of Jesus Christ, I believe there is great power in living authentically as a Christian in every aspect of life, including sales and business. Christian principles and obedience create good character. Your character is instrumental to building trust with your customers and that will deepen and strengthen over time. This deep-rooted character leads to wise decision-making which will ultimately determine your long-term success in sales. When your identity is deeply rooted in God, it empowers you as a salesperson to have passion, live confidently, and sell like no other.

For some reason, we've been conditioned to think our relationship with God and our work life should live in two separate silos, as if who we are as Christians should be set aside when we step into the professional world. We were created by God for his purposes (we are His sons and daughters!) and everything we do should be informed by that reality. This is great news and is a very powerful truth. When lived out, this idea frees us to perform at our best and makes us better in sales.

From the world's perspective, sales can often be seen as an unethical and manipulative profession. I would argue that this occurs when people work from their own strength—without the power of God and without a good baseline of ethics, principals, and morals—and there have been plenty of examples that can be used to justify that perception. That being said, when your business practices are rooted in faith, I believe sales can be one of the most fun, noble, ethical, and rewarding industries in which to build a career. Sales, when done correctly, helps others achieve their goals and fixes their problems through your products, services, and solutions. Helping is really at the core.

I believe God calls us to be excellent in our work and personal lives and to live confidently from our relationship in Him. It's my strong opinion that faith, *plus* the very practical sales advice in this book, will help you soar higher and achieve greater success in sales than if you simply had sales training alone. We are human beings after all, and we were made for a purpose, one that is much larger than what we even realize. When we live properly and authentically *from* our faith, we can fulfill our purpose, WIN BIG, and excel in sales and life. With that said, let's jump into the first lesson on how to be Relentless in Sales!

CHAPTER 1

MENTORS

"What Difference Can Mentoring Make?
All the Difference in the World!"
– Bob Biehl

As I began thinking about next steps after the failure of our company, I sat down with John, a very successful businessman, mentor, and family friend, at a local coffee shop in Winter Park, FL. To this day, John is still one of the most successful small business owners in the history of the Central Florida/Orlando market. He was a member of my dad's church growing up and was always someone I greatly respected and admired. His interpersonal skills, strong business acumen, and sales ability are as good as it gets.

After thoughtfully listening to my story, he gave powerful advice that significantly impacted the trajectory of my early career. He told me that if I wanted to figure out what I should do next, I needed to focus and build off my strengths. John had these words for me: "Definitely go into sales. You are good with people, and genuinely want to help others; I can't see you sitting in an office all day! Working with people and sales in general seems to fit your skill set well. To maximize your potential, get into medical device sales and start selling capital equipment."

Boom! It was as if a light turned on and I was given new hope for my career. John gave me very specific and direct advice. At that point in my life, I really needed this straightforward and wise guidance. I had very little money to my name and the pressure was building as I was getting married to my soon-to-be wife, Sandra, in a few months. Additionally, I had a serious case of feeling "behind the growth curve." All of my friends from college had a head start as their careers seemed to be flourishing and progressing. I was regretting my decision to jump straight into entrepreneurship right out of college instead of joining the corporate world like they did. Eventually, I would realize how truly grateful I was to go through the journey of starting my own business, but at that moment all I felt was pressure to stabilize my career.

I was adamantly determined to make something of my life. I had a deep drive to be successful, just like most young professionals, and I needed to find a career path that was both meaningful *and* could help me provide a good living for my future family. After doing some reflecting and thinking, I followed John's guidance, and coordinated with medical device recruiters to further my journey down the road of sales. It wasn't easy, but I eventually broke into medical device sales with a highly esteemed Fortune 500 company.

Charlie Jones, an author and speaker on leadership and personal growth, often said, "You will be the same person in five years as you are today, except for the people you meet and the books you read." I believe there is a lot of truth in that adage, but I would actually take his statement one step further: If you don't proactively seek to learn from good mentors in your network, you're missing out on maximizing your personal development.

So, read the books, make connections, network, and pray for wisdom, but also **seek out people you respect, and engage with them on a deeper level.** Learn as much as possible about their journey and how it can help you grow personally and professionally. Make the time to truly listen, think, observe, and grow. Bob Goff put it this way: "The fact is, we don't need more information; we need more examples. Stay close to a few people who understand how to resist distraction and direct their energy toward their most lasting purposes, and some of this intentionality will rub off on you."

I feel very fortunate that my father, Pete Alwinson, a.k.a. "Chief," is one of the greatest mentors and friends in my life. Chief was a full-time pastor for the majority of my life, and he has always been a dynamic communicator whose influence has made a huge impact in my development.

People often ask me, "What was it like growing up as a PK (an acronym that stands for 'Pastor's Kid')?" They usually ask this with a slight grin and a curious look on their faces, keenly aware of the often-justified stereotype that pastor's kids are wild and rebellious. I always smile back and tell them that Chief and my mom Caron did a phenomenal job of giving my siblings and I the space to learn about God on our own and did not force religion on us.

Reflecting back, I am very grateful for the gifts my parents gave me. Unlike a lot of parents whose focus is on earning as much money as possible to give their children nice things and a large inheritance, my parents' focus was in a different direction. Their aim was to teach me character and valuable lessons that would help me strengthen my walk with God and succeed in my life and career.

Chief understood the emptiness of only running after money, so he gave me a much more powerful gift that didn't involve money at all. You see, he knew my brother Joel and I were not going to follow in his same pastoral footsteps. What Chief *did* give us was his unconditional support, his commitment to our development, and access to his deep network of loyal friends and a supportive community. Chief gave me the gift of **mentors,** many of whom would help develop me and build a lasting impact in my life. Very early on, he made it a priority to connect me with wise men and women who were successful in business and equally so in their spiritual life. During my late teenage years, he would often pull me aside after church and say "Jonny, that guy over there is a very successful businessman. Go ask him to lunch or coffee and, if you can set up that meeting, I'll pay for it." It was often intimidating having to ask these successful people if they'd meet and talk with me, but I also had confidence knowing my father was someone these men respected. I mean, after all, were they *really* going to say no to the pastor's kid?

All jokes aside, I look back at these experiences and I'm extremely grateful for the skills learned during this time. My dad pushed me to seek out people who could help me grow as a man and, unbeknownst to me, a professional. Networking, building relationships with others, and communicating one-on-one with successful business professionals was instrumental in my early development. Many of these men are still mentoring me to this day.

The importance of mentors to sales professionals, regardless of sales tenure, **cannot be overstated**. When we find a mentor who is committed to our success, we have a significant advantage in our sales career. No matter your age or sales tenure, do you have a person you highly respect who you can call when you need advice or want to improve? Is there someone you can talk with who has been through the challenges you're facing now and successfully managed and overcame them? If not, start today by taking inventory of the people in your network you respect. Think of people career-wise that are exactly where you want to be someday. Look for people both inside and outside of your place of work. Summon up the courage to connect with them and ask to meet up regularly with that person. Do not try to overly formalize this process. It complicates things, can sometimes be awkward, and can hurt more than it will help. I often find people are more than happy to meet with you. Successful people normally like to help others become successful. Discuss a full range of topics, not just business, including personal, financial, spiritual, physical, and social topics.

As sales professionals, we tend to be laser-focused on making money and career progression. This is often especially true when we are early on in our professional careers and HUNGRY for success. We can become so obsessed with our work that we miss the topics that are more important during these mentoring sessions. Thinking with a long-term mindset, living with character, and developing meaningful relationships with mentors are the things that will help you build your career on a solid foundation.

Over the years, I've made it a priority to create a "Board of Directors" for my life. I highly encourage you to do the same. This would be a list of three to five people you highly respect who have high character and ethics and have accomplished in business and life what you would like to accomplish someday. These individuals should also be people who you believe care about your well-being and have your best interests at hand. Developing this "Board of Directors" for your life should take time to create. Slow down and don't rush this process.

With your "Board of Directors" in place, you'll have a wealth of wisdom and experience to lean on for advice as you navigate the uncertain path of life. When you are unsure of your next step, having a team of people you respect and who are invested in your development is a game-changer. One important thing to remember, though, is that unlike God, people—even those who are closest to you—will eventually let you down at some point. Even the best of people will sometimes not come through. That's a human reality. God should always sit at the head of your "Board of Directors" table as He is the "friend who sticks closer than a brother" (Proverbs 18:24).

Enjoy this process! Take a morning or weekend to think it over and then start to learn from credible people who can make you better as a person and also in your craft. Having a mentor can be life-changing. If you take the time to develop your personal Board of Directors, you will greatly benefit in sales.

You can't go far in the game of sales if you go at it alone. You need others, you need different perspectives, and you need the advice from those who have gone before you to help you along the way. Finding a mentor is the first step to developing sales greatness.

Key Lesson:

Are you trying to do everything on your own? You will fly higher and go much farther when you learn from others, especially those who have accomplished what you'd like to do in life. Mentoring makes all the difference in the world personally and professionally.

Action Step:

Who in your network would be a good candidate for a member of the "Board of Directors" for your life? Make a short-list of potential people and then say a quick prayer over your list. Call or reach out to one person this week to schedule lunch or coffee within the next two weeks.

Thought to Consider:

Most people who read this will think, "This is good advice" but will not act on this message either because of their ego or fear. If you truly have the desire to WIN in sales and in life, this should fuel you to take action on building the Board of Directors for your life. It will give you a *significant* competitive advantage.

CHAPTER 2

IDENTITY
The Foundation of Success

"If our identity is in our work, rather than Christ, success will go to our heads, and failure will go to our hearts."
– Timothy Keller

"Jon, you need to "live *from* your identity, not *for* your identity." **This is the phrase that changed my life**. I'll never forget where I was. I was driving in South Georgia working for a new medical device company selling a very disruptive and exciting new technology. I was on a MISSION to become the top Territory Manager in our organization and had a BIG chip on my shoulder to prove my worth as a salesman, because my professional career up to this point was not going as I had envisioned. After my failed entrepreneurial venture and two and a half years selling as an "Associate" Territory Manager, I was ready to prove I had what it takes to run my own sales territory. I was dead set on a "if it's meant to be, it's up to me" mentality.

Growing up as a Christian, I knew better than to put my complete identity in being successful at work. But if I'm being honest with myself, my priorities were a little out of order. I was intensely focused on being the best Territory Manager in my company and God and my family were taking a back seat. A key member of my Board of Directors, my dad, sensed something was wrong and graciously called me out.

"Jon, I sense your priorities are a little off. Remember you are a son of the Most High God. Go live *from* your identify—not *for* your identity. Go pursue excellence and win that Territory Manager of the Year Award, but remember, it doesn't change your identity in God. Never forget that. You have what it takes because you are an Alwinson and you are God's kid!"

I knew he was right and I needed to change my perspective on success. As my dad spoke those words to me, a feeling of freedom, confidence, and faith flooded my veins because I knew my identity was MUCH bigger than any professional success I could achieve. And that was freeing!

When we can truly understand this concept of being worthy and "enough" just as we are, it becomes one of the most powerful and liberating lessons for all people, and *especially* for us sales-people. It doesn't soften you or make you weak. In fact, it does just the opposite! Think about a time in your life where you were completely "worry-free."

For me, a good example is from sports. When I think back to my days growing up, I was obsessed with basketball and you could find me playing morning, noon, and night! Most of the time, I wouldn't describe myself as calm and "worry-free." I was usually a little anxious and hyper-focused before I played a big game. On the occasions when I thought too much or played too hesitantly, I simply underperformed. Can you relate? However, there were plenty of nights when I was care-free, my shot was hitting in warm-up, and I played relaxed like I had nothing to lose. On *those* occasions, I usually put up double-digit points, had way more swagger, had FUN, and played my best games. The difference was obvious! When we have our identity properly aligned in God, it frees us to give our best and keeps us from obsessing about the results so we can rest in our identity as sons and daughters of the Most High God. Remember, you are God's kid (no matter your age), and that will never change.

My pastor, Louie Giglio of Passion City Church here in Atlanta, has made a big impact on how I understand identity. Louie had an awesome message recently that was entitled "True North." In this message, he talked about how we can have a renewed mind when we have our identity fixed on Jesus Christ. One of Louie's key points during this message was "my opinion of me should be growing out of *God's* opinion of me." God loves us and thinks we are awesome. If you are fortunate to have kids of your own, you understand that feeling to a degree, but guess what? God loves us much more!

What does this have to do with sales? Everything! When our opinion of who we are is firmly built on the foundation of Christ, we have a HUGE competitive advantage in sales. It separates us and makes us different. It creates a confident, humble, and like-able spirit that allows us to create authentic and lasting relation-ships with our customers. This is something that the mainstream sales leaders and business professionals either don't mention or don't even understand. Society has a way of conditioning us as business people not to talk about God. But God is our great Hope, Strength, and Refuge. Why shouldn't we talk about Him when we have such a **powerful advantage** when we put our trust in Him? This hope and power is not something we should hold on to ourselves, but openly talk about and share with others.

So I say to you as my dad told me, go pursue those big awards, hunt greatness, be bold, but remember that your identity is being God's beloved son or daughter *first*. No matter your age or what you've been through in life, you have what it takes because there is a God who loves you and has a BIG plan for your life.

Now, go get 'em!

Key Lesson:

Remember: everything flows from your identity. Identity builds confidence. "Live *from* your identity—not *for* your identity." You've already won if you belong to Christ!

Action Step:

Write the phrase "Live *from* your identity" on a 3 x 5 card and keep it with you all week. Read it multiple times per day.

Thought to Consider:

Think back about a time where you felt most "free," connected to God, and in a "flow-state." As you suit up before your next important sales call, think about your identity, smile big, and walk into that meeting with the power of knowing you are a loved son or loved daughter of the Most High God. There is nothing better!

CHAPTER 3

GO ALL-OUT

"The path to success is to take massive, determined action."
– Tony Robbins

Life is way too short to not try your very best. When you *finally* get your chance … you have to go *all-out*. This is the number one piece of advice I give every aspiring up-and-coming sales representative or new sales rep (regardless of sales tenure) who wants to make an impact with their new organization. Had I not given everything I had when I earned my chance to become a full-line sales representative, there's no way I would have the incredible opportunities that I have today. There is a very short window to make an impact with your organization and my advice is always to start FAST.

Adversity has always played a big role in my professional career. I started my career working five years in a start-up that was incredibly challenging and exciting, but ultimately was unsuccessful and failed. I moved on from there into the medical device industry working as an "Associate" Sales Territory Manager as my way to break into the medical device space. Living in Atlanta, there were days as an associate where I would receive a phone call on a Monday afternoon informing me I *had* to fly to a neighboring state for a 7am surgery case in the Operating Room the very next day. I'd literally be sitting down for dinner with my wife and have to tell her, "I need to leave and head to the airport now!" The first 7+ years of my professional career were filled with adversity and challenges like that, and it came with very little financial compensation. I would have to earn my stripes if I wanted to make it.

So when I *finally* had the opportunity to run a sales territory of my own, I was HUNGRY like a dog on the back of a meat truck. This was my opportunity and I wasn't going to miss my shot. I felt I had so much to prove that there was no way I was going to give anything less than my very best effort. If I failed, it wasn't going to be because I didn't give it everything I had to be successful.

The short version is this: I left a Fortune 500 medical device company for a "no-name" startup. When I joined the organization, we had 50-55 outside sales representatives covering the entire United States of America. This company had a strong visionary CEO and a senior leadership team who were determined to do big things. I saw huge potential for me to succeed there, but it was also a huge risk leaving my current company and moving to another startup. I joke when I explain that I left the "Nike" of medical device companies to shoot my shot at this very small organization. At first, I was worried that I made a huge mistake. The cultures between these two companies were drastically different. The previous organization had fostered an extremely competitive culture and this new one was more of a family environment. It was certainly a bit of culture shock from what I was used to and I wondered if I'd succeed in such a different setting.

Despite the nagging feeling that I had made a huge mistake, I didn't wallow in self-pity or begin to feel sorry for myself. The decision to move had been made and if I was going to succeed where I now was, I knew I had to give it everything I had. I could not fail again.

By the grace of God and phenomenal coaching and developing from Justin (you will learn more about him in the next chapter), I threw everything and the kitchen sink at being a successful salesperson. I was able to earn a Rookie of the Year Award in my first year and a Territory Manager of the Year Award in my second. This accomplishment allowed me to win the prestigious "Founders" award, given to the territory manager with the best combined two years in a row.

Although having those two years of back-to-back sales success was amazing, success is *not* the lesson or message I want to get across here. At the end of my Territory Manager of the Year run, the small medical device company I was working for was acquired by a much larger organization. Only a handful of salespeople nationwide were brought over with this larger acquiring organization. This type of acquisition is often referred to as a "tuck-in acquisition," as the larger company already had a stellar sales organization with little need for most of our salespeople. The lesson here is this: had I not given an *all-out* effort over the 24+ previous months with this company, there is no way I would have had the opportunity to be one of the few fortunate individuals chosen to continue with the new company. It was an opportunity that catapulted my career forward.

The lesson is simple. Tomorrow is not promised to anyone. We are only on this earth for a short time. The world of sales (and business for that matter) is a fast-paced environment. When you focus on personal excellence and giving work your ALL, you won't lose. You simply do not know when the next opportunity to take a leap forward will happen and you have to be ready! Going *all-out* means when those opportunities arise, you are poised to take hold of them and put in elite effort to win.

If you get nothing else out of this book (although I'm hoping you learn a great deal), the one thing I want you to walk away with is this: you must keep a **relentless mentality** to win at sales and life. In sales, it's wise to map out your career, but you must keep a year-to-year perspective, understanding that the only thing you are promised is constant change. Organizations will continue to grow, fail, go out of business, get acquired, and CHANGE. Those who stay ready, trust God, and put in excellent work will rise to the top. That's what I want for you. It's why I wrote this book.

At my core, I believe this deeply. It's amazing how *effort* can create distance and a competitive advantage between you and your competition. Adversity and grit combined with a never-give-up mentality have been the story of my career. It's the only thing I've ever been able to control.

When it's all said and done, I probably won't be known as the smartest or most strategic person in sales. But if there's one area I won't ever allow someone to beat me in, it's my effort. Remember that incorporating an *all-out* mentality means doing the right things consistently over time. Putting forth elite effort means being disciplined, committed to serving your customers well, living with integrity, and giving your best each and every day.

Key Lesson:

There are times and seasons in life where you need to put on blinders and give your sales career your best. Early on in your sales career and when you are new to an organization (the first few years) is definitely one of them. These are pivotal times to give an *all-out* effort.

Mentality Tip: Once you've seen the results of going *all-out*, use that experience to push you to never let up too much. Yes, your effort level will fluctuate during various stages of your career, but once you establish yourself as an elite performer, your effort should always stay at an elite level.

Action Step:

Take a weekend to plan and think over your career. Go to www.JonAlwinson.com and download the "Weekend Planner" and consider where you are right now. Is it time to go *all-out* or make an adjustment in your career?

Thought to Consider:

Everybody's Sore.
Everybody's Tired.
Everybody has an excuse.
Don't be Everybody.
   - Lewis Caralla

CHAPTER 4

CONFIDENCE

"Confidence comes from discipline and training."
– Robert Kiyosaki

"You just have to be REALLY confident."

"*…Just confident?* That's it?" I responded.

"That's it, bro!" responded my new manager and future mentor. "Sales is only about one thing – confidence. You have to instill that *feeling* with your customers, build trust, and make them feel confident in YOU as *their* salesperson. Customers want to buy from people they like and trust. Just be yourself bro."

Justin was my second medical device manager and up until this point was the first one who I truly felt cared about me and my development. He was driven, and was several steps ahead of me in the game of sales and life. He was confident, cared about his team, and had an infectious personality. People were drawn to him and being around him made me want to level-up my game so I could get to where he was. He was also very funny and understood how important it was to make your customers laugh.

His jokes were hilarious (sometimes borderline inappropriate) but he used his people skills and humor to develop deep relationships with the customers we served. Justin's impact was critical in my early sales career and helped me understand an important rule of selling—you have to *choose* to be confident and learn to build trust with your customers so they will believe in *you* as their salesperson.

In my experience, it's very common for salespeople to be on one side or the other of the confidence pendulum. More often than not, I see salespeople who are overconfident (arrogant) or who lack confidence (self-doubting). I know this well, because I've lived on both sides of this continuum. Sales can be a very tough industry and people can often get hardened and arrogant by the fast-paced and high-pressure environment in which we work. On the flipside, they can get so beaten up that they begin to soften, run low on motivation, and drift toward mediocrity.

Good sales organizations post and send out their national sales numbers, stack ranked from the top salesperson to the last on a daily basis. This can lead salespeople to feel their worth to the organization is *only* measured by one thing: their sales performance. In order to overcome and thrive, we must find a way to build healthy confidence as salespeople. I've found that building confidence from your strengths, understanding and developing a spirit of humility, and committing yourself to highly productive working habits will put you on the path to building a healthy sales confidence. I want to briefly take a look at each of these elements.

First, building confidence from your strengths is crucial. There are multiple personality and strengths-based tests out on the market today. I highly encourage you to take as many as possible. These tests help you develop a deeper understanding of how God has hardwired *you* personally. Everyone has different strengths and the key is figuring out what yours are so you can lean into them. When you identify your strengths, you should double down and put effort into maximizing those gifts.

It may seem like your focus should be on improving your weaknesses, but to the contrary, research shows that most people will not drastically improve their weaknesses over time. Putting our energy into improving our weaknesses has some value, but even if we succeed in improving our weaknesses, we have merely become "not deficient" in those areas, at the expense of atrophying our strengths. But when you are aware of what your strengths are, you can lean into what you're uniquely good at and turn those strengths into your personal superpowers. Doing this, you can gain more self-awareness and start building healthy confidence because your strengths help you win.

In the Bible, Romans 12 talks about "not thinking of yourself more highly than you ought" and goes on to discuss how each of us has unique and different gifts. This is a great passage to memorize and refer back to, early and often.

In my role as a sales manager and people leader, the very first step I take in coaching my salespeople is to understand how they are wired. I will usually have them take a strengths-based test so I can learn the "cheat codes" on how to customize my coaching to best develop them.

A good example of how I coach to strengths is comparing someone who rates high as an *Achiever* vs. someone who is hard-wired in *Competition*. Typically speaking, Achievers thrive best as salespeople when they compare their progress vs. themselves (You vs. You). Conversely, someone who is hardwired in competition likes to see how they stack up and compare against others at all times. If you coach an Achiever by constantly comparing their performance to others on their team, they will burn out and won't maximise their Achiever strength. However, if you coach, encourage, and challenge this salesperson to exceed their numbers from last month or last quarter (i.e. compete against themselves), they will make the most of this Achiever strength and be more fulfilled, encouraged, and uplifted in their work.

Socrates is often credited for coining the phrase "know thyself." "Knowing thyself" is a huge and powerful competitive advantage when it comes to sales. At this stage of the game, I'm often aware of my strengths and weaknesses. Sometimes I catch myself falling into one of my weaknesses. By simply being aware of them, I can make an on-the-fly adjustment and auto-correct.

A good example of how I apply knowing my own strength is that I have a deep hardwiring for accomplishment and I'm impatient with inaction. I'll often catch myself being far too impatient during a meeting or customer interaction. By simply reminding myself to slow down and stay present, I'm able to get a little better each day. The more we have self-awareness of our strengths and are honest about where we need to improve, the stronger and more confident we become.

Humility is the second key building block in bolstering our confidence as salespeople. As Tom Reilly, in his book *The Humility Paradox*, writes: "As a student of humility, not an expert, I have neither all the right questions nor answers about humility. There is no authority on humility, only students and interested readers. We are all travelers on a journey to discover more about this foundational virtue. Humility is a foundational virtue because it supports all other virtues."

Humility is very difficult to define but is often very recognizable when we see it in person. Wayne Mack wrote, "As soon as we think we are humble, we're not; as soon as we think we have it, we've lost it." Most Americans are taught to be humble; however, I think humility is often misconstrued. Merriam-Webster defines humility as "a freedom from pride and arrogance." C.S. Lewis defined true humility as "not thinking less of yourself, but thinking of yourself less." I believe it is important in every aspect of business and life. St. François Fenelon wrote, "We must learn to take a humble position in *every* situation. We must never brag about ourselves, and especially not our goodness or special strength."

Although I have a long way to go on the humility journey, I try to remind myself of this daily *especially* before engaging with customers. Take a minute and try to think about the people you like to be around in your personal life. People who are arrogant, self-centered, and unlikeable are usually quickly uninvited to personal gatherings, aren't they? The same is true about us as salespeople. If customers don't like you, they will find a way to "block you out" and not work with you. I've even seen customers willing to pay more just to not have to deal with certain sales reps. The antidote is thinking back on your identity (Chapter 2), fueling up with positive intent, and focusing on what you are grateful for each and every day. This puts life in the appropriate perspective and lays the foundation for a humble life.

Adam, one of the key leaders in the organization where I work, exhibits humble confidence in an amazing way. He's one of those guys that has a true understanding of this principle. He intentionally seeks to understand, thinks in terms of the best interest of others, and always keeps the customers we serve at the forefront of his decision-making. I remember a meeting where Adam said, "It's amazing what we can accomplish when nobody cares who gets the credit." This humble and hungry spirit draws people towards you and helps you connect deeply with customers.

Confucius wrote, "Humility is the solid foundation of all virtues. It is certainly a solid foundation upon which to build your life." Tom Reilly put it this way: "(Humility)—a word that masquerades as self-deprecating meekness is a powerful strength. Humility does not change one's personality; it helps align priorities." As you continue on the journey of becoming the very best salesperson and businessperson you can be, remember to make humility an authentic core principle of your life.

Finally, committing yourself to highly productive working habits and daily effort helps build and grow your confidence. And it starts *first* in your mind. Jeffrey Gitomer and his legendary sales book *Little Red Book of Selling* has made a very big impact on how I see sales. It's usually one of the first books I recommend to others who are new to the industry. Jeffery puts it this way: "Believe you can. Have the mental posture for success. Believe you are capable of achieving it. This belief must extend to your product and company. A strong belief system seems obvious, but few people possess it. Too many salespeople look outside (for money they can make) rather than look inside (for the money they can earn). Believing you're the best and believing you are capable of achievement is the hardest thing to do. It requires daily dedication to self-support, self-encouragement, and positive self-talk. How much do you believe in you?"

We will talk more about owning the mental game in Chapter 8, but Gitomer is spot-on. When you understand your identity and know God loves you and has a plan for your life, you can foster deep belief in your God-given abilities. You and I were made for action and created to work, but you have to create highly effective and productive habits to excel.

Have you ever watched a boxer or MMA fighter speak with unfiltered confidence before their upcoming fight? I instantly think of Floyd "Money" Mayweather or Conor McGregor as two of the best trash talkers I've ever heard. Yes, a lot of this is sportsmanship and calculated talk to "sell" more pay-per-view purchases. But often this talk flows naturally after they've put in countless hours of work over their careers *and* the effort in their respective fight camps leading up to the bout. More often than not, these fighters are training two or three times per day during these camps in preparation for their big fight. They've checked the boxes and feel extremely confident about their skillsets and the future outcome of their fight. I love every aspect of how good these fighters feel leading up to the fight. As long as we keep our egos in check, we too can create a similar feeling through our daily effort and preparation.

Early in my sales career, I realized quickly that many of my sales counterparts were just as competitive as I was and they too wanted to become the #1 sales rep in the country. What I also realized is that although they *wanted* to become #1, many of them did not want to sacrifice to make it happen and were ineffective in their daily activity. Maybe they had not gone through as much adversity as I had, and possibly they just weren't as disciplined. Regardless, I noticed several negative habits in these salespeople that started to emerge.

One noticeable habit was that they started to slow down and "coast" shortly after lunch time. I observed a great deal of sales reps wasting time calling each other, networking, and complaining about their day. They would call me and I would hear from others that they called them as well that day with the same rants about their day and how frustrating their customers were to deal with. How did they ever get anything done? These salespeople would get distracted and waste large amounts of times wallowing in self-pity. I hated listening to these calls, so I intentionally made a personal rule to combat this complacency. My rule was this: to screen all internal sales reps phone calls until 4pm, every day. I would not allow other salespeople to pull me down and waste my time, my paycheck, and my future. I was committed to staying focused and keeping my effort high—every single day.

This gave me an enormous amount of confidence. When my peers were slowing down for the day around 1pm, I was just getting going by attacking the second half of my day. As I pushed through my day, I intentionally tried to make several more sales visits and aimed to make at least three to five more sales calls per day. By not giving into the temptation to slow down after lunch, I simply had more hours in the day toward my goals. The result? My confidence grew, I created distance from my peers and reached new heights along the way. If you want to truly be great in sales, stay disciplined on the work at hand, create highly productive working habits and put in world-class effort!

Key Lesson:

Confidence comes from building on your strengths, developing a spirit of humility, creating highly productive working habits and putting in elite sales effort.

The more self-awareness you have, the more you can grow as a salesperson. Be genuine and real with others. This creates humility, which will give you a pleasant and likeable spirit to win with your customers.

Action Step:

Take a personality test, spiritual gifts test, or strengths-based test today. Then review it with someone you respect and admire. Get their opinion as well.

Thought to Consider:

"In the fear of the Lord one has strong confidence."
  - Proverbs 14:26

CHAPTER 5

RELATIONSHIPS > EVERYTHING

"If you want others to like you, if you want to develop real friendships, if you want to help others at the same time as you help yourself, keep this principle in mind: Become genuinely interested in other people."
- Dale Carnegie, *How to Win Friends and Influence People*

The longer I'm in sales the more I am truly convinced it is ALL about building good relationships with your customers. It's about putting their needs first, not yours. Hopefully you are either working for an organization or have created an organization that has a customer first mindset. Ideally, you have a product or service that truly helps fix a problem or fills an important need for your customers and end users. If you don't believe in the company you work for and the products you represent, move along quickly to another organization that you can truly get behind. Life is way too short and your customers can instantly tell if you believe in and are passionate about what you sell and the organization you represent.

One of the best people I've ever seen at connecting with others is Big Jim. Big Jim was a member of our church growing up and a close personal family friend. Jim is a big man, with a huge warm smile and hands the size of a small grizzly bear. Jim wasn't loud and obnoxious; he was quite the opposite. Jim had a huge smile and a calm and confident demeanor. His personality was contagious. He'd shake your hand, hold onto it for a long period of time, and pull you in for a big "dude hug." He was always happy to see you and listened intentionally when he spoke with you. Big Jim always had a huge grin on his face and was always ready to tell you a funny story. He'd make good eye contact and ask you genuine questions that made you feel important. That's what great relationship-building looks like! Are your customers happy to see you like I was when I saw Big Jim?

Even if you are in an industry where everything is highly transactional, fast-paced, and unfriendly, it's YOUR job as a salesperson to be the difference maker, create the relationship advantage, and improve the environment around you. A smile is a powerful weapon; it lightens up the room and tells others what you expect from them in return. Smiling big with your customers, although a seemingly minor and easily overlooked habit, is a difference maker to getting your relationship with your customer off to a great start.

Take a minute and think about the best salesperson you've ever met. I'm sure they are intelligent, have a good sense of humor, are confident, and have key objectives for every selling interaction, right? What else do they do? The best that I've seen never jump right into business with their customers. Even when their customers try to jump straight to business with them, the best salespeople I've encountered have mastered the art of "pulling the conversation back to relationship" *just* long enough to connect with their customers at a relational level before jumping into the business at hand.

The next thing they do is **listen**. Listen, listen and listen some more, then ask some really good questions based on what they heard. It's the salespeople who focus on the needs of their customers first vs. leading with their own agenda that WIN. Think about any major purchase you've made in your life: a new car, house, boat etc. What was that experience like? Was the sales professional helpful? Did they ask good questions and try to put themselves in your shoes before offering solutions?

The reality is most salespeople are not good at this. Ask yourself, how can I truly help this customer? Have I created some commonality and legitimate rapport with this customer? Do I understand their needs and what their true pain points are? Am I offering solutions that truly benefit them? If not, start there and really try to find out where you can add value and adjust your message to serve their needs first. Remember great salespeople are problem solvers.

The best practical advice I've received on connecting with your customers is to intentionally think of each customer as an old friend you haven't seen in a long time. Imagine how excited, warm, and happy you'd be seeing them after an extended time away from each other. That smile, that feeling, and attitude is exactly what you should take when approaching your customers! It takes intentionality, centering yourself, and mentally creating the right mindset, but it pays HUGE dividends. Be sure to intentionally connect first and warmly build relationships, just like Big Jim!

Now to the fun part. Meeting with customers and developing relationships with your customers *is* the fun part! That's where we finally get to show what we are made of and begin developing meaningful relationships and advancing business with your customers. I liken sales to playing sports. It's like game day every day you are in sales and it's fun to try your best to put "points on the board" every day.

If you are a high energy person like me, it can be very hard to slow down and plan prior to running into your accounts. I've been known to be a bit of a cowboy and shoot from the hip at times, but thanks to some great mentors, I've found it is critically important initially to slow down, gather all the facts, and think strategically before you go rushing into meeting with your customers. In Chapter 7 we dig deeper into planning for your territory/assigned sales geography.

Having well-intentioned motives is the next important step when approaching your customers. Your customers are just like you and they can recognize if you are genuine or not. If your motives are good and you approach the sales relationship with positive intentions, you will be received well. However, if you are self-centered and have greedy intentions, your customers will instantly pick up on this, push back, and keep their guard raised. The key is being humble, open-minded, and customer-focused when discussing your products and services. If you've really listened to your customers and identified where their needs are, this will come naturally to you. Be sure to fuel up daily with positivity so you can genuinely reflect that attitude when interacting with your customers.

When meeting with customers, I routinely say, "If you get nothing out of today, I want you to know we truly care about working closely with your organization, providing value, and getting our working relationship off to the right start." Some salespeople might laugh or put down this approach, but it's genuine to me and it helps me authentically be my best self as a sales professional. Most of the times in sales and in life, it's not what you say but how you say it that matters most.

After you've had your initial conversations and interactions with your customers, consider doing what Scott, a mentor of mine, does. He's built a successful career in part by consistently sending handwritten notes. By going "old school" with a handwritten note, you'll be making it clear to your customers that they are worth your individual time and attention.

It's crucial to keep reminding yourself to make it ALL about your customers and make them the heroes throughout your sales process. Donald Miller wrote an amazing book called *Building a StoryBrand*, and it's been extremely helpful along my sales journey. In his book, he outlines how to make the customers the hero of the journey, not ourselves or our organizations. Donald says, "When we position our customer as the hero and ourselves as their guide, we will be recognized as a sought-after character to help them along their journey." Donald's point here is that when we recognize that our customers are the hero in their story, we aren't worried about centering ourselves and competing for who will be the main character in our interaction. Instead, we can take the role of the guide that helps lead the hero through whatever obstacles are put in front of them. I've found this to be a game-changer and very important paradigm shift to make.

I'll never forget a time when I was working with a large account that loved our products but they needed help with economic savings. Linda, their manager, expressed her desire to make a deal happen but needed appropriate savings. We ended up finding a win-win with our partnership through a combination of expanding our market share with the customer and savings, but what stands out to me most is not the terms and conditions of the agreement, but rather how big she smiled and how our relationship deepened when I intentionally highlighted her strengths to her CEO. I remember genuinely telling her CEO, "You know I cover multiple states and work with a lot of managers like Linda, but her creative ability here to make this deal happen is why we are here today. She is one of the best I've seen." You think Linda was happy with me? You bet your bank account she was! I was genuinely impressed with her, openly shared that sentiment with her boss and as a result have developed a genuine and deep relationship with both her and her CEO to this day.

You see, when we make it about others (by truly putting their needs first), adding and giving real value, we win. Maybe not during the first meeting but eventually you will establish yourself, your company, and your products as the best solution for your customers. When we make it about ourselves, we limit our impact and are not nearly as successful in sales. I've had the privilege of selling in the medical device industry for years. I love what I do and the customers we serve through our physician and nurse caregivers. By listening to my customers and always putting the patient first, intentionally trying to best understand their clinical needs prior to offering any products or solutions, it creates an environment where we rightfully make them the hero and begin to establish credibility.

Genuinely trying to identify a hero in each account can take different forms but I always try to approach this with sincere intentions. People can often be overlooked and underappreciated in our business. More often than not, the folks that clean the medical technologies we sell are just as critical to patient care as the physicians and nurses that directly treat the patients. I intentionally focus on developing deep relationships with ALL the individuals we get the privilege of working with, not just with the physicians. Not only is this something I am hardwired to do, but it really is fun building real and trusting relationships with individuals at all levels of the organizations you serve. When you find individuals who are truly "heroes" and highlight them within their organizations, you find great joy in helping others *and* you move from being just a salesperson to a true business partner and hopefully, a friend. Be generous with your praise when you find something praiseworthy – it costs you nothing and can do wonders at building amazing relationships.

Warning: Be sure to approach your customers with good intentions and do not try to manipulate them or act outside your authentic self. If behaving with a customer-first mindset isn't genuine yet, hold off until it becomes part of who you are. Reflect back on Chapter 2 (Identity), take a weekend off to think over your approach with your customers, and start again. Remember, your customers are just like you and can smell bad intentions a mile away.

Key Lesson:

Building relationships like Big Jim, listening intentionally, and making your customers the heroes is the winning formula.

Action Step:

How can you get a little better today? Refer back to this chapter often, think through these principles, and set a "calendar reminder" to remind yourself to put your customers first. This is an important habit and skill you must develop.

Thought to Consider:

"If you work just for money, you'll never make it, but if you love what you're doing and you always put the customer first, success will be yours." – Ray Kroc, Founder, McDonald's

CHAPTER 6

DEVELOP AN ELITE SALES PROCESS

"Create, Advance, and Close."
– Mike Weinberg

I love talking about the T's and C's of an elite sales process. I think it's absolutely fascinating to watch how people take an idea of selling a product, service, or solution all the way through the entire sales journey with a prospective customer. To me this is both an art and a science.

The science of sales involves the skill set and knowledge that help make salespeople successful. There are hundreds of techniques that have been developed through trial and error by talented sales professionals for many years. The art of sales is harder to define and even harder to teach. It's the soft skills and sales intuition about doing the right thing in the right moment that develops in salespeople over time. This is highly-nuanced (oftentimes subjective) and I've found that you typically pick this portion up from experience and observation of other really good salespeople.

What I want to focus on in this chapter is the science of sales, the **skill** portion of a highly effective sales process. What I've discovered is that great salespeople have a deep understanding and a consistent "structure" of how they go from pre-call planning (idea generation) all the way to closing deals and following up with the customers they serve. They have an **elite sales process**—a highly effective and repeatable process broken down into the steps they use to sell products or services.

Great salespeople understand that most selling situations are different, but they adjust and adapt their sales process to best serve the needs of the customer and accomplish the goals of the customers they serve and organization they represent. This framework allows elite salespeople to have clear understanding throughout the sales process to ensure they serve their customers well and consistently advance their products or services.

The best sales process training for me was early in my sales career when I worked for my first medical device company. I went from four years of selling shoes to selling a highly sophisticated and complex medical technology platform used for neuro, spine, ENT, and orthopedic surgeries in the operating room. This was a HUGE jump from selling shoes, and there was a steep learning curve.

Looking back, a key discovery I made was if you do not have a very concrete and sound sales process, it is very difficult to find consistency in sales. Furthermore, a good sales process gives you the ability to assess and understand *exactly* where you are in your customer's buying cycle. That's crucial, because if you don't know where you are in the process, you won't know where to go next.

If you develop an elite sales process and a deep understanding of sales, you can sell anything! It doesn't matter if it's a box of erasers or a million-dollar piece of medical equipment. The timeframe and buying process might be different, but the steps throughout the process should follow a consistent pattern.

An effective sales process is the light that helps guide and direct you throughout the sales process. As a passionate basketball player growing up, I see a good sales process as similar to having good shooting form in basketball. The more consistent your form is, the more likely (with proper repetition and practice) you will consistently make shots. Just like basketball, sales is a fast-paced environment and each shot is unique and different. Not only does having a highly effective sales process provide consistency during every sales engagement, it also helps you understand *exactly* where you are throughout the process and intuitively know what you should do next. This chapter will help you develop a consistent and effective sales approach.

So what makes a sound and highly effective sales process? I was very fortunate to have really strong sales training early in my selling career. The training I found most helpful came when I had the privilege of attending a MATRIX (MX®) Achievement sales training event. This was and still is the clearest and most fundamentally sound sales teaching I've ever experienced. With the permission of the author, Todd Zaugg, the steps in the MATRIX (MX®) Sales Process are the following:

1. Pre-Call Planning

2. Approach the Customer with Rapport

3. Identify Pain

4. Demonstrate Value

5. Advance the Sale

6. Close—Ask for the Business

7. Follow-Up

As we dig into each aspect of an effective sales process, remember the words of Jeffery Gitomer, "The question shouldn't be, do I know this? The question should be, *how well do I do this?*" No matter our experience or sales tenure, we all have the opportunity to sharpen our skills and get better every single day. With that said, let's jump straight to it!

The first step in every sales process should always be some form of **pre-call planning**. The more successful you want to become as a salesperson, the more time you should take in researching your prospective customer. Do your research on both the organization and the individuals/stakeholders within the organization you are calling on *before* picking up the phone or driving to visit the customer. This is especially important when you have a limited number of customers you can sell to in your assigned territory or geography. For example, if you have only 40 customers, every interaction—especially the first few—are critical. It's crucial to spend time and thought on what your conversation might look like prior to engaging your customer.

Look up the customer's website and pay close attention to the "About Us" page. Look at their mission statement, core values, administration/staff, and assess what is important to them (5-10 minutes minimum). It's amazing what a big difference it can make when you incorporate a phrase, photo, or quote from their website into your conversation or presentation. It will often earn you their respect and helps align your offering with what matters most to their organization. Additionally, if you are not looking up your prospective customer on **all** the social media platforms, you are simply missing out. What if the person you are meeting with has the exact same hobbies or interests as you do? If you knew that information going into the meeting, don't you think being armed with that information would give you great ideas for relationship-building during the meeting? Without a doubt!

Social media can be a wealth of information and insight into your potential clients, so make sure you are taking advantage of the information they are sharing with you. But be careful not to get stuck in the "scrolling trap" during work hours. Social media is intentionally designed to trap you and can waste your time during the work week. You must be disciplined when using this to look up a prospect. I like having a military mindset when using social media – get in, get the information you need, and get out as soon as possible. Pro Tip: do your pre-call planning outside of peak selling hours. Doing so allows you to maximize your selling effectiveness during the day and calmly study your customer outside of the rush of the business day.

After scanning their website, double-check your company's CRM (Customer Relationship Management) for any important historical data or previous customer meetings. If your organization doesn't have a CRM, stay organized and start to build your own via an Excel document (more on this in Chapter 7 about how to create a Zoned Territory for your sales territory).

The last thing to note about pre-call planning is, in my experience, as both a salesperson and as a sales leader, that most salespeople overlook the importance of this first step. Some salespeople surprisingly skip this step completely! Although this is a very easy step, it is usually very hard to stay consistently focused on making it happen. As salespeople gain more experience, they often become overconfident in their abilities and start to "wing it" in their meetings. I would strongly encourage you, no matter your sales experience, to not fall into this trap. Stay disciplined! If you are one of the few that can get really good at pre-call planning, it will separate you from the pack and you will rise to the top.

The next step in developing an elite sales process is **approaching the customer with rapport**. Dale Carnegie's timeless book *How to Win Friends and Influence People* is in my opinion one of the best books ever written. This book is a must-read (and continual review) for every salesperson. Two sales characteristics stand out when approaching the customer with rapport. The first part of rapport-building is found in Chapter 2 of his book where he discusses how people instantly smile when they meet a dog wagging its tail. The powerful example of having a genuine smile is game-changing when it comes to sales. In highly transactional industries, relationship building can be difficult. But it is just as critical today as it was a hundred years ago. The importance of building relationships will never change. Just like Big Jim from Chapter 5, be warm and take the time to focus on developing relationships.

The second part of rapport building is being genuinely interested in other people. I will often pull back the conversation and focus for a few minutes on relationship-building. Tell the customer you are looking forward to the conversation today, that you have everything prepared, but actively engage and be genuine when you are getting to know your customer. Ask where they're from; engage and be inquisitive about their family and hobbies. Having pictures ready on your phone of your family, your kids, or pets is always wise especially if they ask you similar questions. Relationship building is HUGE and many salespeople overlook this critical step. Smile big and be intentionally warm, authentic, and interested in *their* life.

The third step is to **identify pain**. Pain, or "areas of opportunity," is why we as salespeople have jobs. At the simplest level, we are problem solvers. Pain is usually the only thing that gets your customers to "move" and buy from you. Your customer has a need, and you as their salesperson have a product, service, or solution that can fix or alleviate their pain. When I am hiring new salespeople, I look to see if they have some structure of a sales process. I'm not too picky when it comes to the exact process they use, but I am picky when it comes to their understanding of what gets customers to move and "buy" —i.e. pain. Do they have the experience to know that we are problem solvers, and it's our job as salespeople to put ourselves on the same side of the table as our customers to fix this pain? Normally this comes with experience. As I like to say, "It takes a number of years of getting kicked in the teeth" before this realization occurs.

After identifying pain, **demonstrating value** or the *solution* to the pain you are solving comes next. For example, if a customer tells you in confidence that they are having trouble keeping payroll accurate and up-to-date, and you sell payroll services, your antenna is probably going up. This is the moment that separates the good from the average and the elite from the great. Asking *more* questions at this stage is critical. You don't want to assume you know what's going on here.

Many salespeople fall short at this point. Many jump to how they can immediately solve their customer's pain before they fully understand the extent of this pain. "Tell me more," "help me understand," and "what effect does that have on your organization" are phrases that you should start practicing. SLOW DOWN. At this step you need to take the appropriate time to figure out the pain before offering up your solutions. After you have a deeper understanding of your customer's pain, roll out your offerings, services, and solutions to your customer to see if working together would be a good "fit."

Advancing the sale is when you as the salesperson can start taking control:

> "Mr./Mrs. Customer, you mentioned that in XYZ areas you are having trouble and that _____ (this expressed need) is where you need some help."

At this step, be confident in yourself (Chapter 4) and diligently show your customer the "next steps" of working together and how your offering can alleviate their pain. Here's where your personality and the "art of sales" really comes into play. If you have an abrasive personality or are overly dominant, you might turn off your customers at this point. However, if you've truly built rapport, are smart, helpful, and have uncovered their needs, you can truly shine. Remind the customer of the pain they expressed and how you as the salesperson feel confident that your product, solution, or service is best suited to resolve their problem. Ask and demonstrate for them the appropriate next step, schedule a follow-up appointment, meeting, or call right there on the spot, and advance the deal to the next logical step. For many salespeople, that might be asking for the order or setting up a product demonstration or evaluation.

The subsequent step is **closing** or **asking for the business**. I'm a big believer in demonstrating real value before asking for the business. This is the fun part in sales! It's where your heart rate is increasing, you've proven the value you can bring to their situation, connected the dots for the customer to see how your solution solves their pain, and built rapport so that they are receptive to working with you. Now is the time to make a direct ask for their business with confidence, knowing your hard work and skillful sales process have set you up for your best chance of success with this customer. Simply recap and outline your value during your close. Express what you've discussed at this point:

"Mr./Mrs. Customer, you mentioned _____ is causing frustration and delays in your business (*pain*). As we've discussed, if _____ (*pain*) continues, _____ will continue to occur and limit _____ in your business. That said, I feel very confident if we follow these next steps _____ (outline your value and clearly defined next steps), then _____ (show them how you can alleviate their pain)."

Here you simply need to recap your total value offering and next steps. Don't overthink it! Be genuine, BE YOU, and show them you have a sincere desire to help. Your customers will connect the logic of using your product/service with the better customer service and working relationship you offer, and you will set yourself up for success. As I conclude meetings, if all the boxes have been checked, and after I've outlined all the steps of my value offering mentioned above, I will often say,

"Mr./Mrs. Customer, I am confident this is the right thing for you and your organization. We discussed all the advantages. What do you say? Let's do this!"

This is my favorite way to close. You can read it in their eyes. Ask them if they agree and confidently (not arrogantly) lead them forward. If you've done everything right, you are actually helping them, providing more value than their current offering, and in some cases saving them from their current reality. There is no better feeling than helping others find the win-win in sales.

Key Lesson:

Having a well-disciplined sales process will consistently and more predictably allow you to win. Don't be robotic about it, but rather flow from step-to-step. A good sales process is the foundation to winning consistently and best serving your customers.

Action Step:

If you and I were at a coffee shop sitting together and I asked you to flip over a napkin and write down your sales process in a simple, bullet-point format, could you do it? Practice that today.

I encourage you to pick a sales process that works for you and work at mastering it! Remember, it's like your shooting form in basketball—if your form is inconsistent, your shot will be too. The same goes for your sales production.

Thought to Consider:

Mike Weinberg, author of *New Sales. Simplified.*, coined the phrase: "Create, Advance, and Close." A great sales process will help you do just that.

CHAPTER 7

ORGANIZE FIRST, THEN TAKE MASSIVE ACTION!

*"You do not rise to the level of your goals.
You fall to the level of your systems."*
- James Clear

Early on in my sales career, I was training at a facility in Nashville, TN. Between training sessions, I was connecting with colleagues and discussing best practices with managers and other sales reps within our sales organization. Dave, a very successful regional manager, pulled me aside and asked me if I'd created an organized document outlining all the account details for all the accounts I worked with in my territory. I tried to play it cool, but I was a little confused.

"Umm yes, but what do you mean exactly?" I asked.

He asked, "Do you have an Excel document created with a list of ALL your customers, geographically-organized, with the key contacts of your customers, all the products they are ordering now, and the potential or "upside" products you have the opportunity to sell them?" I was stunned, because I realized I had nothing created that was remotely similar to what Dave was talking about. Although I attempted to play it up that I had something "similar" created, it sparked a fire in me and helped me realize that if I truly wanted to become a great salesperson, I needed to get my stuff together and get extremely organized.

Immediately after arriving home from training, I rushed to my office and went to work, creating and implementing what I later called the *Zoned Territory Sheet*. This document has been the lifeblood for me both as a Territory Manager and as Regional Sales Manager. This document is very different from using a CRM (Customer Retention Management) software. Although there can be some overlapping details in a CRM, the *Zoned Territory Sheet*, when printed, is geared more towards helping you stay laser-focused and organized on winning new revenue in your accounts. It outlines your key contacts and stakeholders but most importantly, helps you stay hyper-focused on the new revenue upside/opportunities within *each* account. This document should be a living and breathing part of your day-to-day, updated and printed out weekly and sitting shotgun in the front passenger seat of your car.

My favorite part of this tool is it helps organize these accounts according to where they are located in the geography of your sales territory. For example, if you are in the Northwest portion of your territory, you should bundle and organize all these accounts and their respective account information in that particular "Zone" (i.e. the Northwest Zone). This helps you during your sales engagements to ensure you are not overlooking an account in a particular geography and helps you compartmentalize your sales territory.

I've found that you know you are maximizing this tool well when you have coffee stains, pen marks, and notes written all over this document on a weekly basis. In today's high-tech environment, printing anything out on paper is often frowned upon. However, my rationale for printing and updating this document on a weekly basis is because it helps keep you FOCUSED. I'd imagine you are just like me, and anytime you pick up your phone, there's a huge chance you will get distracted. Having a formal, printed document keeps you intentionally away from your phone and all the distractions within: text messages, social media, notifications, and other phone apps. This helps you to stay locked-in and committed to production during selling hours.

My recommendation is that you update this document at least once a week with all the data you collect from calling on your customers and prospects. I recommend updating this at the end of the week before you head into the weekend. You can go to www.JonAlwinson.com to download a free *Zoned Territory Sheet* template and watch a tutorial video on how to organize this tool.

After creating your *Zoned Territory Sheet*, the next step is to understand which customers you should focus on during your selling hours. Our time is our scarcest resource, so it's incredibly important to spend it on areas where we can see the highest return. One of the main principles I live by is "your best customer is your existing customer." I always start there. So, who is your best customer? Most salespeople instantly know who their top one to five customers are, as they have the largest market share and largest annual spend within their sales geography. For most sales organizations, as these accounts go, so goes your sales territory. So it's important to grow and protect these customers first. Social scientists refer to this concept as the 80/20 Rule or the "Pareto Principle." This principal helps you understand where to focus your efforts and time to have the greatest effectiveness. It states that "80% of your results come from 20% of your efforts."

As a sales professional, you should always have a stack-ranked list of your top customers, their performance year-to-date, and listed product areas you need to protect and grow your business. The *Zoned Territory Sheet* helps with that. Many of the salespeople I lead have added an extra column in their *Zoned Territory Sheet* next to the customer/account name to let them know the ranking of each and every customer (i.e. #1 Customer in Annual Spend, #2 in Annual Spend etc.). This helps you keep first things first and heighten your awareness on your most important customers.

After developing your *Zoned Territory Sheet* and listing your best customers from first to last, I recommend creating a very simple and straightforward *Weekly Attack List*. Early in my career, when I was in contention for being the top sales rep in my company, I found I could only relax on Saturdays. Most people think I'm crazy, but I've never liked the idea of anyone outworking me during the week. So, Saturday between noon and one in the afternoon was my weekly planning session. I was relaxed, usually just finished with a workout, and able to calmly build out and think deeply about my schedule for the next two weeks. Additionally, I could review the information I wrote down from my weekly meetings with customers, update my *Zoned Territory Sheet* and write out my *Weekly Attack List.*

Typically, what I would do was write down all the opportunities I *thought* I could close or advance in the next two weeks. I'd write everything out and then ask myself, "Jon, from a gut perspective, what opportunity has the very best chance of closing this week?" I'd circle that opportunity and label it #1. Slowly and methodically, I'd work my way through the list. After thinking deeply about my territory, I would finally re-stack rank my list from highest probability to close to least likely to close and systematically work those calls and visits in throughout my week, checking off and celebrating the wins along the way. The key here is to commit yourself to becoming organized and create a time during the week where you can relax and consistently plan out your week. If you make this a habit, there will be a compounding effect where you will get better and better each and every week. Organize first, then attack!

The next important aspect of being a highly organized salesperson is to ensure you have your sales documents and sales samples, along with your vehicle, consistently organized *every* week. Many of the individuals reading this book, like myself, are in outside business-to-business sales. Your sales tools, product samples, and personal car/vehicle are the lifeblood of what you do. Just as your physical appearance is an important part of your presentation to your customers, ensuring you are fully prepared with your sales samples and marketing sell sheets and having reliable and clean transportation is instrumental to your success.

As a sales leader, I've seen countless representatives who had excellent interpersonal skills but were ill-prepared with their organizational skills, which ultimately prevented them from having maximum success. Many of these individuals have earned very prestigious accolades, however many never developed the discipline and organization needed to be elite. Looking back, had they mastered this skill of organization, who knows what great heights and success they could have accomplished. Don't let that be you! Commit to excellence when it comes to organization. I recommend having at least a one-hour-long planning session with yourself each week.

I would highly recommend setting a calendar reminder to ensure you don't skip a planning session. Other tactics I would suggest is using the "Delayed Send" feature in your email/ Outlook and set it to send out first thing Monday morning to ensure you don't bother anyone in your internal organization or prospective customers over the weekend. This allows you to take massive action and outwork your competition while not stressing out those in your network in the process.

Finally, make sure your car is clean and ready to go each week. You should be regularly scheduling your oil changes, filling up your gas tank, and cleaning the inside and outside of your vehicle on a weekly basis. This is SO important. If your car is always cluttered and messy, this is oftentimes an indication that your inner world is not organized. Stay sharp, be a true professional, and ensure you are able to sprint into the upcoming sales week. Stay locked in, organized, and ready to go!

Key Lesson:

Organize, then attack. The best salespeople have a system for staying organized.

Action Step:

Work on creating your *Zoned Territory Sheet* and *Weekly Attack List* today. Just take action and you will be amazed at the impact this will have on your business.

Thought to Consider:

Abraham Lincoln once said, "If I only had an hour to chop down a tree, I would spend the first 45 minutes sharpening my axe." I would add that you should do this planning before or after key selling hours. This will maximize your productivity.

CHAPTER 8

OWNING THE MENTAL GAME

"The two things in life you are in total control over are your attitude and your effort."
– Billy Cox

Your success as a salesperson is largely dependent on how you **think and control** the mental aspects of the game. From one perspective, it's one of the most exciting, fun, and liberating industries in the world. You don't have to sit all day in an office and feel trapped. You are simply asked to go out, meet with your customers, build relationships, produce, and you will have the opportunity to earn uncapped income. When you think about it from that perspective, sales is a beautiful industry! On the other hand, you are constantly stack-ranked and judged on your performance vs. others, you face constant adversity, and challenges and problems arise on a daily basis.

Salespeople are often reminded of that old adage, "You are only as good as your last day/month/year of sales." I've seen very talented salespeople self-sabotage throughout the years because they didn't take the time to develop the mental toughness necessary to persist and thrive in the game of sales. In order for you to conquer the mental aspect of sales, it's critical for you to document your personal wins, create effective daily disciplines, and push yourself physically, spiritually, and mentally to build healthy standards of excellence in your life.

One of my best friends, Nate, has been in the sales game for a long time. It's been helpful having him in different sales industries than me as it's allowed us to compare notes and share advice with one another throughout the years. Our friendship has become an "iron sharpens iron" type of relationship (Proverbs 27:17). At one point in his career, Nate reached out to me with some challenges he was facing. Like most salespeople, Nate began selling a very price-sensitive piece of technology in a unique economic time and was feeling like he was falling into a "sales slump." He wasn't making sales like he had in the past and needed a brother to talk with. (Side note: having a trusted friend in your life like Nate is really encouraging because it allows you to be there for each other and help each other through the sales game as needed. Be sure to find a peer to push you as you begin building your sales career.)

"Jon, I'm not putting points up on the board like I'm used to doing," Nate winced as we sat back in our chairs while our families were swimming at our community pool. "It's frustrating. I'm starting to question if this job is right for me." More importantly, Nate was starting to question himself.

"Nate, think of all the success and quota attainment you've had over the years with the different organizations you've been a part of. It hasn't been easy, but you are a GREAT salesperson. Not average, not just good—GREAT. Brother, remember and take note of all the wins you've had along the way. This will help you through the hard times."

I could tell these words "hit" and landed at the right time for my friend. It's mutual encouragement, unity, and friendship that we need to share with each other in order to push ourselves and be successful in sales. From there we talked deeper about documenting our wins and learning to reflect back on what effort, focus, and lessons we took to earn that success. It's not good enough to talk about them, you need to write them down!

Whether you are new to sales or have been in the game a long time, the first step in developing your mental toughness is to *document your wins* so you can remember them. If you are new to sales and do not have any wins to document, think back to your early family life. Think through all the sports you played, hobbies you engaged in, and any times you were really proud of yourself. Write your life accomplishments down and think through what you are grateful for. For me it was starting a lawn mowing company with my older brother, my academic accomplishments, and times in sports where I scored the most points or put forth a tremendous amount of effort. No matter how big or small those accomplishments seem, they are the building blocks upon which you can begin to build your mental fortitude.

David Goggins, a retired NAVY SEAL, ultramarathon runner, and overall legend of self-discipline, uses a mental image of a cookie jar to accomplish this same concept. Goggins keeps an imaginary cookie jar in his head, and into that cookie jar he places his past accomplishments and victories. When he's struggling in a task and needs to remind himself of what he's capable of, he can open the cookie jar and see many examples of when he fought hard battles and won. That gives him the motivation to keep tackling the problem at hand. You can use the idea of a "cookie jar" in your own life too! It's easy to focus on the negative and forget the many ways we have succeeded and overcome obstacles, but if you can remind yourself of your victories, you'll be a step ahead in winning the Mental Game.

My next recommendation to winning the Mental Game is to create effective daily disciplines so you can grow mentally tougher and more resilient each day. The great news about discipline is that it's a habit. It's something that can be learned and improved over time. The most impactful daily discipline I've ever incorporated is the discipline of waking up early. I've found that if I wake up early (5 a.m. or earlier), everything else in my day is better. The first thing I do upon waking is drink a lot of water and a couple cups of coffee (don't judge my coffee addiction!). During this time, I make sure I spend time with God, reflect on my identity (Chapter 2), read the Bible, review my goals, and practice mental affirmations. Below is an example of my morning schedule, my goal reviews, and my daily affirmations:

Schedule:

5:00 a.m. – 5:30 a.m.: Wake up, drink water and coffee, then begin the day with prayer and gratitude.

5:30 a.m. – 6:30 a.m.: Read Bible, review my agenda for the day, do daily affirmations, and close in prayer.

6:30 a.m. – 7:00 a.m.: Spend 30 minutes working on my craft. Read business/leadership and sales books, and go through industry-specific material/articles.

7:00 a.m. – 7:30 a.m.: Cardio and strength train, then stretch (usually listening to a podcast).

7:30 a.m. – 8:00 a.m.: Shower and get ready to attack the day!

Goal Review Example:

- 5-out-of-5 Years Consecutive Sales Plan Achievement on or before Dec 25th 20__.
- Help Lead My Team to a Region of the Year Victory on or before December 25th 20__.
- Exceed Quota by $1 Million on or before December 25th 20__.

Affirmation Examples:

- P.G.F. —Put God First. "I Will Put God First Today!" – Louie Giglio
- "God is with me, God is helping me, God is guiding me." – Norman Vincent Peale
- "I'm fully prepared for this."
- "I got this!"
- "I will come through on this."
- "As I improve, I am helping others improve."
- "I've done this thousands of times before."

- "I don't fear. I don't care what you think. I don't care what I think. I only care what God thinks."
- "Everything great comes with my willingness to risk."
- "I play BIG!!"
- "I will play BIG TODAY!!"

For more examples, go to www.JonAlwinson.com for lists you can download for yourself.

The next important aspect of developing mental toughness is exerting physical effort and developing a lifelong physical training program. Physical training is a very important component for developing mental toughness. That's why athletes typically have great foundations to develop in sales. Not only does physical training look attractive to your customers, it creates a mental fortitude to persist when times get tough. Athletes typically develop the discipline of waking up early, showing up early (15+ minutes early for practice), and developing healthy diet and fitness routines. Andy Frisella, owner of 1st Phorm Supplements and creator of the popular discipline routine "75 Hard," always says, "Discipline is a skill." It's something that can and should be developed daily and increased over time.

Finally, in order to own the mental game, you have to build the proper mental framework for success. The first step in this process is caring *less* about what others think about you, and this has been one of the hardest areas for me. Like many of you, I generally want people to like me, and I *especially* want my customers to like me. Having your identity rooted in God (Chapter 2) is the foundational key to growth here because it gives you the freedom to care less about what others think and more about what God thinks of you. Proverbs 29:25 says, "Fear of man will prove to be a snare, but whoever trusts in the Lord is kept safe." The more we grow in putting our identity in God rather than imperfect and highly flawed human beings, the more power and growth we make in developing the proper mental (and spiritual) framework for success.

Over the years, I've learned to improve my self-awareness, create processes, and grow in this area. I've created daily checklists (I call them *Power Lists*), created annual goals, and written down the playbook for my life as a habit I've built over time. I highly encourage you to do the same. These tools help me to properly orient myself so I can care less about the opinions of others and put them in the right perspective.

Famous Clemson football coach Dabo Swinney put it this way, "Don't worry about criticism from people that you wouldn't seek advice from." I love this! Put the important things first and continually remind yourself to trust God, love your family, and always look at the source of the person giving you any type of feedback. If the comment has no legitimate logic, simply smile and move on. God's got you!

Key Lesson:

In order for you to conquer and own the mental side of sales, it's critical for you to document your personal wins, create effective daily disciplines, and push yourself physically, spiritually, and mentally to build healthy standards of excellence in your life.

Action Step:

Carve out one hour and start writing down your personal wins, how you can create effective daily disciplines (physically, spiritually, and mentally), and in what areas you can begin to care less about others' opinions of you.

Thought to Consider:

My view of me is growing out of God's view of me. Therefore, in every interaction today and this week, I can have confidence that God loves me and is developing me.

CHAPTER 9

CONQUERING FEAR

"Inaction breeds doubt and fear. Action breeds confidence and courage. If you want to conquer fear, do not sit home and think about it. Go out and get busy."
– Dale Carnegie

Growing up as a pastor's kid, I've heard countless sermons and very impactful messages around faith and fear. Despite having strong personal faith, great training, and lots of knowledge, fear (if I'm being honest) is something that is always lurking right around the corner for me. When I find myself giving into fear, I remind myself that faith is the only antidote strong enough to conquer fear.

Last chapter, I mentioned Proverbs 29:25, where King Solomon wrote, "The fear of man lays a snare, but whoever trusts in the Lord is safe." Every time I read this, I am reminded of how I can allow other human's opinions to put a stronghold on my actions. It is literally a deadly trap to trust in others' opinions of us in business and in life. In this context, "fear" is not physical but rather a physiological fear.

As a people-person, I am usually energized when I am around others, and more often than not, I enjoy being around others. I've also been raised in the school of hard knocks and have seen a great deal of negative situations happen in business. I've watched as deals that appeared to be perfectly executed figuratively and literally go up in flames (just ask me about a certain piece of medical technology I used to sell!).

Fear is a very real feeling that we must continually work through. As I've aged and have developed more self-awareness, I've found myself asking: "Am I being my authentic, true self? Or am I behaving this way to get the approval of others? Am I living from a position of fear rather than faith? Am I being my real self or acting a little timid or self-conscious in order not to lose or gain this business?"

Countless times when I've put my trust in people over God, I've been let down. Period. In the context of sales, fear can become an overwhelming and debilitating issue if we don't put it in its proper place. Remind yourself of your identity and the confidence that it brings (Chapters 2 & 4). Sales is a mental, emotional, and spiritual game. Adopting a faith mindset centers you back to what's important and allows you to enter your meetings with customers with power that only flows from an All-Powerful God.

A great way to conquer fear in sales is scripture memorization. (Side note: repeating scripture out loud to yourself has a powerful side benefit of helping you with communication. Studies have also shown it helps improve your IQ. That said, I highly recommend you memorize and repeat scripture out loud.) One of my go-to verses is Romans 8:31. This verse says **"If God is for us, who can be against us?"** See how empowering that verse is if you can really allow yourself to believe it? The Bible is full of wisdom like this that can help you overcome the fear you're experiencing. If you find yourself in a state of fear, try repeating this verse out loud along with other encouraging verses over and over. By telling it to yourself, you are reminding yourself of the truth that you do not need to be afraid. Through repetition, the words will begin to move from your mouth to your heart. Trust God and ask Him to help you break through the stronghold of fear in your life.

One of my best friends, Jonathan, told me that he repeated 2 Timothy 1:7 to himself over and over again throughout his tryouts for the police academy, and that it made a huge difference for him during that process. The verse says, "For God has not given us a spirit of fear, but of power and of love and of a sound mind." Speaking things like this to yourself can have a huge impact on helping you conquer fear and move forward with courage!

I've also repeated a phrase I picked up over time: "I don't care about what you think; I don't care about what I think; I only care about what God thinks." This has been a very helpful mantra that has stuck with me through the grind of sales and centered me on what's important.

Norman Vincent Peale was an American clergyman best known for his book *The Power of Positive Thinking*. Mr. Peale had old tapes on positive thinking that have played a big role in my early sales career. There was a phrase that stood out to me that helped me break through a season of fear I was experiencing. Dr.

Peale encouraged his listeners to repeat this phrase until they started feeling better: "God is with me; God is helping me; God is guiding me." I still can hear Dr. Peale's piercing voice repeating that over and over again. It's really made a profound impact in my life and is still something I use to this day. Fear can be such a big part of sales (and life), but when we live from our relationship with God, it frees us up to become our true selves, not panic over deals, and pursue excellence in our work!

The final piece of practical sales advice to break through fear is simply to take massive action. More often than not, salespeople wallow and dwell in their mistakes and fear instead of brushing themselves off and picking up the phone to call on another customer. I've experienced this firsthand from individuals I've coached, and during the peak of my selling years. Salespeople can be perfectionists and can often get really upset when we make mistakes.

Growing up as a basketball player, I had to learn quickly to "reset" my mind after a bad shot and to move on to the next play. When I was pushed outside of my comfort zone and made a bad shot, I had to find a way to reset my mind and move on. "CLEAR!" I would repeat, sometimes out loud, but usually in my head. I'd also say "Next Play" so I wouldn't sulk in my frustration and embarrassment. Owning this mental game is just as (if not more) important in sales than it is in sports. Sports end at some point for most of us, but business and sales last a career.

Early on in my sales career calling on hospitals and surgery centers, I would make dozens of customer calls. Many of these calls were utter disasters as I fumbled over my words or was cut short and hung up on. I'd often laugh it off after those calls, shake my head and say "Next Play." Immediately, I would make another call instead of letting myself wallow in self-pity. I knew if I allowed a bad call to break me, I would not grow as a professional or as a person. Never allow fear to hold you back from achieving your goals.

It wasn't until I became a sales manager that I saw how widespread fear is in the sales world. I thought it was just me, but fear is a natural human condition we must all self-manage to perform at our best. Taking massive action, reminding yourself of your identity (living *from*, not *for*), clearing your mind from a bad play, and picking up the phone and making the next call will set you on your way.

Grant Cardone, in his masterful book *The 10X Rule*, talks about how taking 10X action can give you the confidence to go for your dreams. I love when Grant says, "What if the only thing standing in the way of your greatness was that you just had to go after everything obsessively, persistently, and as though your life depended on it?" Grant is a polarizing figure and wildly successful. He's written some great books and I think his content is generally spot-on. When you remove fear and take massive 10X action, it allows you to live confidently in your identity in God, which is *key* to success in sales.

Author and leader John Maxwell talks about a time in his life where he was "stuck" due to uncertainty and an overwhelming sense of inaction. He decided to take out a pen and write the phrase "I am responsible, I am responsible, I am responsible" hundreds of times before he was able to break free from his debilitating fear. If fear is holding you back, I encourage you to grab a pen and do the same!

What's stopping you and holding you back from breaking through the stronghold of fear? What limiting beliefs are holding you back from accomplishing great things for God, for your family, and for you personally? Now is the time to break through, now is the time to tell your family you love them and you are GOING FOR IT. Now is the time to believe in your God-given talents and abilities. And remember Romans 8:31: "If God is for me, who can be against me?" Let's go!

Key Lesson:

Choose to be a person who is not debilitated by fear. Commit to doing things like memorizing Scripture, finding helpful affirmations that allow you to "reset," and taking massive action to eliminate fear as you pursue excellence in your career. Here are some suggested verses:

"... do not be anxious about anything, but in everything by prayer and supplication with thanksgiving let your requests be made known to God. And the peace of God, which surpasses all understanding, will guard your hearts and your minds in Christ Jesus." - Philippians 4:6-7

"For I am the LORD, your God, who takes hold of your right hand and says to you, Do not fear; I will help you."
- Isaiah 41:13

"For God has not given us a spirit of fear, but of power and of love and of a sound mind." – 2 Timothy 1:7

Action Step:

Write down either an affirmation or piece of scripture you appreciate. Put it on paper and keep it with you all week. Read it as much as possible out loud. Sure, some people might think you are crazy, but just think of that as training to care less about what others think about you as you strengthen your faith muscles.

Thought to Consider:

"Action attacks fear; inaction builds fear." – John Mason

CHAPTER 10

THE SKILLS OF GREAT SALESPEOPLE

"Superstars are relentless, unstoppable prospectors. They are obsessive about keeping their pipeline full of qualified prospects. Unstoppable and always on."
– Jeb Blount

In addition to being excellent relationship builders (covered in Chapter 5), successful salespeople ask good questions and listen deeply. They also understand the health of their business, spend their time wisely, and remain persistent and optimistic as they pursue their goals.

After you establish rapport and start down the road of building a meaningful relationship with your prospective customers, learning to ask good questions and listening deeply are very important skill sets you must develop. You've heard it said before, but truly take the time to put yourself in your customers' shoes for a moment. What are *their* goals? Yes, I know you need to advance your organization's agenda and close new business for your organization. That's a given! But what about your customers? What do they want? Until you slow down and truly listen and learn from your customers, you won't know if your product, service, or solutions are a good mutual fit or not.

Early in your professional career, you typically don't think (or care) about the ramifications of starting your working relationship off on the wrong foot. You just want to SELL and prove your worth to yourself and your organization. But as you grow, mature, and develop, you quickly realize that doing business with the wrong customer is draining, time consuming, and a waste of both your time and the customer's time. It doesn't matter how good your sales ability is, if you are routinely putting your energy in trying to sell to the wrong customers, you're just going to be spinning your tires. Therefore, as you initiate with potential prospects and future prospects, take the time early on to listen deeply to ensure doing business is mutually beneficial. Ensure your product, service, or solution is a good two-way fit. Otherwise, you will encounter major headaches and issues.

Those that I've had the privilege to coach know I ask A LOT of questions. I joke and say it's because I am not smart enough to know the answers (which *is* often true), but more importantly I am trying to demonstrate to my team and *teach* them one of the most valuable lessons in sales: don't assume you know what your customer is thinking. You <u>must</u> clarify.

Instantly, I think back to a time where I had my team together in Nashville, TN for a local regional meeting. We were doing a session where everyone was bringing customer opportunities that seemly had reached a dead end. As a group, we were strategizing on how we can bring these opportunities back to life. A newer member of my team was discussing a deal in particular that was more complex than it appeared at the surface, and as she was explaining the issue she was facing, Ben, one of the very talented Territory Managers here in Atlanta, had his eyes on me, knowing what was coming.

"Why?" I stopped the newer teammate in her tracks. "Tell me more" I said. "Help me understand?" I kept digging deeper and deeper with my questions, pushing for answers that soon my newer team member didn't have.

Needless to say, she got a little frazzled realizing how many questions were left unasked over the course of her sales process. Ultimately, this person hadn't taken the time to "gather all the facts" in order to have a good understanding of where the opportunity truly stood.

I looked back at Ben and he had a wide smile on his face. He was holding back his laughter. Ben said, "I ask all those questions myself now and don't assume, because I don't want to deal with those questions from Jon."

We all laughed as a group because everyone on my team had received the same form of grilling questions from me over the course of their careers. I had made a habit of digging deeper and really drilling down with my questions to try to get to the heart of a problem. I looked at Ben and my team and said, "But it works, right?" They all agreed that not assuming we know the answers and digging a few layers deeper are the keys that open up good understanding and meaningful relationships with our customers.

Oftentimes, salespeople are uncomfortable and afraid to ask second- and third-level questions. However, the more practice you put in, the better you get. Be sure to listen deeply with your customers because that's where the learning begins. Most of us know this is true, but how good are we at this? This is often a gut check for most of us because we know we need to be intentional and put what we know into practice. Try asking "Why?" and digging a few layers deeper during your next meeting. That's where the magic happens!

Finally, showing positive and open body language is incredibly important during your meetings. I try to nod my head and make sure I have a positive and warm smile on my face. Sometimes when salespeople think deeply, they look angry, and this can come across negatively to your customers. Try to avoid negative body language, fidgeting, or crossing your arms. We can all agree that these are SUPER basic skills, but I believe the basics and fundamentals *are* the important things, and so often we don't realize the little ways our subconscious body posture affects how we come across to others.

Here's my go-to formula during meetings:

- **Introduction and Rapport.** Get to know your customer. Let them know you are looking forward to the conversation and appreciate the opportunity to sit down and meet with them. (You don't need to overly thank them, but still be respectful. Remember you bring great value—especially if you pre-call planned)

- **Gain Understanding.** Tell them you have a few really good things you'd like to share, but before you share, you'd really like to understand more about their current reality, how they are doing personally and professionally ("What's on their hot plate?"), and what they need right now in their business. My friend, Ryan, likes to ask what their 1-, 3-, and 5-year goals are.

- **Dig Deeper.** After the customer shares, I like to circle back to a point they made in a previous rundown before moving forward in the conversation. "You said _____ is an issue or challenge right now. Can you tell me more?" The key here is to stop and listen deeply with intent. You may only get the opportunity to "dig deeper" on one question, so use it carefully. "Why?" Or "Why has that been an issue or important for you?" After digging, be sure to thank them for that feedback.

- **Engage.** After your customer has fully shared the state of their business and reality, it should feel natural for you to begin sharing and having good active two-way communication on your story, your value proposition, the capabilities of your products/services, etc., and how you provide value helping customers similar to themselves. At this point there should be some very healthy two-way conservation and Q&A. Finally, what would it look like to take the next step together? Follow the advice in Chapter 6 (Develop an Elite Sales Process) and look to prove the value of your solution.

There are a lot of ways to "skin the cat" here, but my hope is that this framework will get you started to creating your own personalized meeting framework.

Next, good salespeople have a deep understanding of their business. They have strong analytical skills to ensure they spend their time wisely and maximize their efforts with their customers and the markets they serve. When you have a deep understanding of the sales numbers in your business, you often spend your time in a very productive and effective manner. Understanding where you are going to get the new revenue generation in your territory and growth is everything for salespeople. The clock is always ticking and the best salespeople always know where they need to spend their time and efforts.

The good news is, most sales organizations have powerful technology to understand current product mix, spend, and year-over-year growth for your current customer base. When you study this information it helps you answer questions like: Where are my opportunities for new growth? Who's up and who's down? Why? What current customers do I need to follow up with? Where can I add value this month, this week, and right now?

Understanding these ordering trends is extremely powerful. Take the time to analyze this information and narrow it down into bite-sized chucks to ensure you don't get overwhelmed but rather encouraged. I would strongly recommend taking this information and adding it to your *Zone Territory Sheet* and *Weekly Attack List* (see Chapter 7).

After five years of really solid performance in my sales region, I was beginning to sense the sales professionals on my team felt like they maximized the growth in their sales territories. I started picking up on comments like "There is not much else I can do!" and "I don't know what else I can possibly sell to them." Despite recognizing they indeed had very strong performances, I knew I needed to do something.

After a long weekend of housework, including washing my house windows, "Operation Squeegee" was born. I remember running to The Home Depot and buying all six or seven window squeegees off the shelf. They were covered in the typical sawdust that I've grown to love from these home improvement stores. I wiped them off, grabbed a marker, and wrote a hand-written note to go with each squeegee. Then I gave one to each member of our sales team and told them we were going to begin "squeegeeing our territories."

Good sales performance can always get better, and we started that day to make sure we were not overlooking a single product line or service to our customers. We started with the analytics and discussed every customer and every product line. The results were incredible! My sales team went from thinking they had no room left to grow their territories to diving deeper with their customers and expanding their market share in just a few months. Their sales growth was a clear sign that Project Squeegee was a roaring success!

Finally, great salespeople are persistent and stay optimistic and focused on their goals. I remember early in my career selling a very exciting and extremely disrupting piece of technology. I was working heavily in the Georgia market and customers were starting to leave the leading market provider to move to this new technology. One evening, I was out to dinner with a physician and my regional manager. The physician said to my manager, "You know, we love Jon. He always has a smile on his face, is positive, and has pushed us about as hard as anyone could … without pissing us off." That was music to my ears. He and his staff liked me—which was good—but he knew I wasn't going to let up. I knew this technology was better for the patient population he served and I was persistent and relentless.

Jeb Blount in his book *People Buy You* says, "If you want to know what your single most powerful competitive edge is, just look in the mirror. That's right, it's you. Do these other things matter? Of course they do, but these are just tickets that give you access to the game. When all things are equal—and in the competitive world we live in today they almost always are—*people buy you*. Your ability to build lasting business relationships that allow you to close more deals, retain clients, increase your income, and advance your career to rise to the top of your company of industry, depends on your skills for getting other people to like you, trust you, and BUY YOU. When you fully accept and adopt that People Buy You philosophy, your confidence will go up and you will perform at a higher level."

Key Lesson:

Successful salespeople ask good questions and listen deeply. They also understand the health of their business, spend their time wisely, and remain persistent and optimistic as they pursue their goals.

Action Step:

Which of these three areas do you need to work on the most? Practicing asking good questions/listening deeply, deepening your understanding of your business, or remaining persistent and optimistic? Pick one area today to work on this week. Check out www.JonAlwinson.com for some additional resources.

Thought to Consider:

"Our greatest weakness lies in giving up. The most certain way to succeed is always to try just one more time."
– Thomas A. Edison.

CHAPTER 11

DAILY HABITS TO WIN!

*"Habits are the compound interest
of self-improvement."*
– James Clear

As salespeople, we are constantly faced with problems to fix, difficult personalities, customer issues, countless meetings, and hearing the word "no" a lot. I've found that in order to thrive through these challenges, you **must *own* your morning, your daily habits, and routines.** Essentially, you need to create repeatable, positive processes in your life to help you grow faster, protect your attitude, and consistently improve your performance. I highly recommend that you start with mastering your morning routine. The reason the morning time is so critical is because, for most people, you are just starting your day and if you get this off to a right start you can really make each day impactful.

The first step in ensuring your morning routine is off to a great start is tapping into an energy source much deeper than ourselves by taking the first 10-30 minutes of each morning to center yourself on God. It's a powerful difference maker that every person needs in order to create long-term success. In and of ourselves, we are weak, fragile, and prone to mistakes. Connecting to God, whom I believe is the Creator of all things and who wants to have a personal relationship and friendship with you, is life-giving. I recommend starting your morning early and developing what Chief (my dad) has coined your Daily Appointment with God (DAWG).

For most people, they smile immediately when they hear the phrase "DAWG" in relation to spending time with God. Although the name DAWG to some may sound like a cheesy or funny acronym, in reality, its simplicity makes it memorable, and we know the best salespeople make things simple and memorable. Ultimately, this tool helps guide you towards remembering your **Identity**, discovering your **Purpose**, deepening your **Character**, and creating massive **Confidence** in your journey with God. Download your copy of a DAWG Guide for free at www. JonAlwinson.com.

The two areas of the Bible I recommend focusing on would be to read a chapter of Proverbs a day and then concentrate on reading a little bit of the Gospels (Matthew, Mark, Luke, and John) each day. Proverbs is chock-full of wisdom about the art of skillful living, which is super helpful both in life and in sales. Because there are 31 chapters in Proverbs and at most 31 days in a month, I recommend you reading one chapter of Proverbs every day. Just follow the calendar and read the appropriate chapter for that day. If it is July 24th, simply read Proverbs 24 that day. To further elaborate on the benefit of reading Proverbs, below are a few examples of its wisdom.

- **Proverbs 13: 3 – "Whoever guards his mouth preserves his life; he who opens his lips comes to ruin."** How good is that? My interpretation: Think about the words you use; they will make you or break you in sales. Words are powerful, guard your mouth, be wise.

- **Proverbs 11:2 – "When pride comes, then comes disgrace, but with the humble is wisdom."** My interpretation: Pride and ego are some of the biggest areas of concerns for salespeople. They can often kill deals by turning off your prospect. Humility is always the winning formula.

- Finally, **Proverbs 15:22 – "Without counsel plans fail, but with many advisers they succeed."** My interpretation: How often are you trying to do it all by yourself and not using your resources and voices of wisdom in your organization?

In addition to spending time with God, I've found it incredibly helpful to create meaningful affirmations in order to build powerful mental, emotional, and spiritual strength for each day. This world can be very negative and can pull us down if we let it. What's the result of your life if you just let it beat you up and pull you down?

In his book, *The Coffee Bean*, Jon Gordon (one of my favorite authors) tells an empowering story that's a good reminder not to be passive in our personal growth. Don't just let the world "happen to you." Instead, take control of your life and your attitude. We can either soften, harden, or make the world better! I've found that mental affirmations fuel us each day to handle the hardship and difficulties that can come our way so we can overcome and influence others in a positive way. H. Norman Wright, in his book *A Better Way to Think*, says:

> "There's one nagging reason that keeps many of us from moving ahead in life. It's our thoughts: those seemingly insignificant sentences that pass through the mind, greatly influencing everything we say and do. From our thoughts we hear messages that can propel us toward great accomplishments and positive change ... or drag us into a negative spiral."

The good news is you are not along ... we are all human and we all struggle with keeping our mindset sharp. So how do we overcome? In addition to reading the Bible each day, start developing a list of positive affirmations (Chapter 8) that will help build mental and spiritual fortitude.

Finally, do you have an organized routine you follow? Do you own your schedule or does your schedule own you? I am a huge fan of Michael Hyatt's "Full Focus" Planner to stay highly organized. This planner has worked wonders to help me stay organized. Not only do these planners present well in customer-facing meetings, they help keep you organized on a daily, weekly, monthly and quarterly basis.

The winning habits I've created with this organizational planner are writing down and itemizing my daily activity from 8am to 5pm and listing out the top three most important tasks that I need to accomplish the following day. By writing down my schedule the night *before*, I am able to wake up and stay on the offensive vs. defensively reacting to my schedule throughout the day. This brings all kinds of focus and clarity to my day. Unless it's urgent, I stay laser-focused on my detailed and thought-through objectives throughout the day.

Key Lesson:

When you own your morning and stay highly disciplined with your daily habits and routines, you elevate your performance.

Action Step:

What area do you need to work on the most? Is it waking up earlier, creating an affirmation list to ensure you are preaching good messages to yourself, or spending time praying to God? Choose one area to focus on today.

Thought to Consider:

"If we wait for the moment when everything is ready, we shall never begin." – Ivan Turgenev

CHAPTER 12

ELIMINATING ENTITLEMENT

*"It's hard to get up at 5am in the morning
when you are sleeping in silk sheets."*
- Marvin Hagler

"Nobody owes you anything." Except he didn't use the word *anything*. He said a four-letter word that wouldn't be appropriate for this book. My older brother has always had a way with words. Often his intuition is spot-on, but the delivery can be blunt and not always intended for the softest of ears.

I've been reminded of this phrase throughout my career. He said it during an important conversation we had when I was in college. I remember sitting around a coffee table with a few buddies talking about what life would be like after we graduated. Joel, my older brother who's a few years ahead of us and much more mature, is a serial entrepreneur and businessman that just happened to overhear us when he walked into the room. "SAY WHAT?" Joel said. One of my buddies repeated the fact that he felt he "deserved" a certain amount of money when he graduated college due to his degree and having graduated from that particular college.

Without hesitation, Joel laid into us. "This is where you guys have it wrong, nobody owes you @#$%," he said. Stunned, my friend immediately started trying to backpedal but also wanted to defend how he felt he was entitled to or at least expected a certain amount of money due to the college we all were graduating from.

"You guys are dead wrong," Joel replied. "In fact, that entitlement is exactly what's wrong with not only you guys but with our country right now. Your reality is not how the world truly works. This entitled thinking is weak and you all need to adjust your mindset." Joel was pointed and direct, and his message hit us right between the eyes. We aren't owed anything, by anyone. When we start believing this fallacy, we instantly begin growing weaker, relinquishing our power, and looking to others vs. looking within.

One of my favorite business people and entrepreneurs, Gary Vee, created a poster that he and his team put up throughout New York City with the phrase "No One Owes You Anything." (The posters even come with little tear away tabs you can pull off and take with you.) This mentality is SO important for us salespeople. When we begin to think our customers and the world owe us anything, we become weak and less effective as salespeople.

To instill this principle, I created a similar document you can print off for free at www.JonAlwinson.com. Download a copy and start fostering this winning mindset today. This is a great daily reminder that we should keep a humble and grateful attitude for ALL the opportunities we have in this world. Start now. Re-adjust if needed, but throw away your entitled attitude. I'm raising my hand right now because I need to hear this message **every single day**.

One of the best minds in sales, Anthony Iannarino, put it this way: "Your enemy is comfort. Once people find a level of income and stability that they find comfortable, many people let up and stop growing and doing what they were doing to get there. Keep hustling. We can't ever let up. Once we get content, we start declining."

This is so true. Years ago, when I had very little money, I installed ¾ inch rubber horse mats in my garage gym. These mats certainly did an effective job of preventing the weights from chipping and cracking the garage floor. But unfortunately, these mats have slightly raised knobs that are extremely uncomfortable to lay on and don't make for a perfectly smooth floor. Even though I could easily replace those mats with commercial grade "smooth rubber flooring," they are a good daily reminder for me to stay tough, to train hard, and to never get complacent or comfortable.

Entitlement is very dangerous—especially in sales. It keeps you in "victim mode" and prevents you from developing a growth mindset because you stop feeling the need to improve. I encourage you to find ways to eliminate feelings of entitlement and continue to incorporate things in your life that will improve your resilience and determination. Sales and life are difficult. If you always feel someone owes you something, you are wasting tremendous time and energy. No matter what level of success you've achieved, I implore you to keep a humble and hungry attitude. Humility combined with a genuine desire to help your customers is the winning formula. The moment we start thinking others owe us anything is the moment we push off onto a slippery slope that leads to mediocrity and weakness. I am preaching to the choir here when I say, be strong and courageous—nobody owes us anything!

Key Lesson:

Entitlement is dangerous. It makes us weak and leads to poor performance and a life of mediocrity.

Action Step:

Take a few minutes to evaluate this important topic. On a scale of one to ten (ten being you live a life free of entitlement), where do you fall? What action could you take to move one notch up on this scale?

Thought to Consider:

"I would like my kids to inherit a world where people succeed because of merit and hard work, not entitlement, and where people accept others for what they are and not try to change them." – Guy Kawasaki

CHAPTER 13

RESPONSIBILITIES OF A SALES REP

"Discipline is the bridge between goals and accomplishment."
– Jim Rohn

Mike Weinberg, author of *New Sales. Simplified.* and *Sales Management. Simplified.*, is one of my favorite sales leaders in business. When I listen to him talk on his podcast, I catch myself saying out loud, "That's EXACTLY what I've been thinking," yet Mike usually describes it in a more eloquent and straightforward manner. Mike has a way of making complex things very simple. Simplifying complex issues and making them easy to understand is an important attribute of great salespeople. In addition to all his practical advice for individual contributors and sales managers, one of my favorite things about Mike is his mentality on sales.

At its core, our job as salespeople is to CREATE, ADVANCE, and CLOSE revenue for the organizations we represent, according to Mike. It's a simple yet profound mantra (Create, Advance, and Close), and it's so good to have leaders like Mike simplifying sales so we don't feel like we need to reinvent the wheel. Ultimately, we are the revenue generators for the organizations we represent. We are the front lines. We build the relationships and are the hunters for our organizations. When salespeople get pulled in many different directions, they drift into mediocrity and often get pulled away from what's really important. If you believe in what you sell and the organization you represent, you will put your customers first and follow Weinberg's advice—Create, Advance, and Close.

That's what it's really all about! However, it's very important to remember that you are not going at this alone. As a member of a sales team, you have a responsibility to help establish a good culture for your team and to also be a student of the game, learning from your teammates. As Dabo Swinney (head football coach of Clemson University) says, learn how to "bloom where you are planted." I want to take a moment to focus on these areas of responsibility.

When I first started in sales, I wasn't a great teammate. I had gone through a lot of adversity the first 7+ years of my career and I was laser-focused on only one person—me! When you are an individual contributor, it's easy to only think about yourself, your customers, and the markets you serve. But if you are self-centered, not only do you "make up a pretty small package," as John Ruskin says, but you also make for a terrible teammate. One of our duties and core responsibilities as salespeople is to help build good culture by bringing positivity to the teams and organizations we represent. This can come in many forms, but just as you should be adding value and helpful insights to your customers, it's your duty and responsibility to do the same to your organization.

Helping to build a good work culture is number one. Are you *only* focused on yourself? What I've found is when we are only focused on ourselves, we limit our professional and personal growth now and career growth down the road. I'm a product of watching others. I've seen career suicide time and time again. Often times it's an individual who did not mature enough past thinking beyond just themselves and working at every attempt to look good in front of others. Spoiler alert, EVERYONE can see it! I've been guilty of this a time or two, and we need to constantly monitor our motives as salespeople.

My Rule of Three when it comes to contributing to and building a good work culture is be **grateful**, be **positive**, and **share ideas** with your team. Most salespeople are part of a team bigger than just themselves, and that means usually the collective good is supreme. It's difficult with competitive and hungry sales reps to create an environment of being collaborative, grateful, and positive, but what I've learned is it's your responsibility. When you help build a good team culture, it actually ends up creating an environment that helps you get better as a sales professional.

One of my wise mentors would always say to people, "Don't be an _____." You fill in the blank, but it's a word similar to jerk. It's on us to put in the personal development work to bring these things each and every day. An author I mentioned previously, Jon Gordon, wrote *The Power of Positive Leadership*, *The Power of Positive Teams*, and *The Energy Bus*. Jon Gordon is also a must-follow on social media, especially LinkedIn. Jon posts consistently on Monday morning with the following:

It's Monday! Today let's:
- Attack this day with enthusiasm
- Stay positive
- Be thankful
- Replace "Have to" with "Get to"
- Be a blessing to others

Jon's positivity and leadership has cemented in me the importance of being a good teammate wherever you are and at every leadership level you rise to achieve. Start today remembering that it's your responsibility to be a great teammate and elevate the culture of your organization.

Sharing ideas is critical when it comes to being a good teammate. As I mentioned above, I didn't become good at this until I became a manager. Think about it for a second and put yourself in your manager's shoes. How do we all get better? How do you make a collective group of salespeople better? The only way is by having a highly engaged group sharing their wins and their losses. As long as the manager has built a team culture that is healthy and open, it's your responsibility to evaluate the things that are working and not working in the field.

As a sales rep in my early days, I would often glean information from others. Unless they asked for feedback, I would hold onto the golden nuggets that worked and were successful. Don't be that person. Proactively and consistently share feedback from the field. It will build your brand, make you a better salesperson, and help the "team" elevate to new heights!

Bringing helpful and practical ideas from the field will help your teammates and organization improve and get better. Teaching these insights will always level you up and will make YOU a better salesperson in the process. When I was a new sales rep, I never shared the key insights I was learning and I kept everything close to the vest. It wasn't until I began managing people that I realized how selfish I was being and how much value I'd been holding back from my teammates. It seems counter-intuitive, I know, but if you want to be great in your current sales role and position yourself for future promotions and next level opportunities, you *must* be a good teammate. Adding to your sales team's culture (bringing positivity) and sharing best practices (what's working and what's not working) is the best place to start. Giving value and teaching and discussing with others makes you better!

It's also very important to always be a student of the game of sales. Early on in elementary school, one of my basketball coaches nicknamed me Jon "The Thinker" Alwinson. Quite frankly, I hated the name when he first labeled me with it, but as the point guard for our team, there was something in me that Coach liked. He liked how I was processing the game, looking for areas to attack, making my teammates better, and ultimately trying to WIN the game.

Looking back, I guess it's how God has wired me, but I am always thinking and always trying to get better and grow. One of the main reasons I wanted to write this book was to help others in their journey too. This field isn't always black and white. There can often be some grey areas. Laws, business ethics, and morals should always be crystal clear and never be compromised, but in sales and dealing with people, there isn't always a perfect answer. Because of this ambiguity, it's so important to always be a "student of the game." Reading everything you can, listening to audio recordings, and studying salespeople you respect are great ways to get started. Find ways to motivate and push yourself out of just being average into being excellent.

John Mason has made a profound impact on how I see life and sales. In his book, *An Enemy Called Average,* John starts off the book with saying, "Your least favorite color should be beige." John links being decisive to "going on the offensive" and "taking the initiative for your life." We have to choose to be intentional for our own development. No one is going to do it for us. That's why its key for us to always be learning and growing.

During the National Sales Meeting of one of the first medical device companies I worked for, they handed us a business card with the quote: "**Out Plan**, **Out Execute**, and **Out Hustle** your competition every day." I think about this often. This mentality wasn't my reality when I first started in sales. It took time to develop and foster. But the more I thought about it, I realized that sales is often about competing. So if I am going to compete, I want to compete to WIN. Studying others, asking good questions of your teammates when you see their success, and devouring everything "sales" related you can get ahold of are great ways to get started. I have a list of great resources on my website. Commit now to a life-long journey of being a student. As William S. Burroughs said, "When you stop growing, you start dying."

Finally, one of my favorite leaders is Dabo Swinney. Just listening to him more than a few minutes makes me want to run through a wall for him. No wonder he's become one of the winningest coaches in recent college football history and has one of the most sought-after programs in the country. If my kid ever had the choice of picking a winning college football program to join, Clemson Football would be right at the top. I've listened to dozens of interviews of Dabo being asked about his success. Dabo consistently repeats the key pillars, quotes, and lessons he learned along the way from others.

First, he cites Booker T. Washington as someone who said, "Do common things in an uncommon way." What a powerful phrase! Dabo helps us see the insight that how we separate ourselves from others and rise above mediocrity and just being "average" is **by being uncommon** among your peers. Go the extra mile, call the extra customer (or five extra customers), and be willing to put in the extra hours. Otherwise you'll just blend into the crowd.

In Proverbs 22:29 it says, "Do you see a man skilled in his work? He will stand before kings, he will not stand before obscure men." Obviously, a man in this context stands for men or women who have sought after greatness and are honored before kings for the excellence in their work. Greatness stands out!

This is a winning mindset that has to be developed and intentionally processed. Dabo Swinney, in his viral YouTube interview with Ed Mylett, goes on to say, "If it's your job to go get the coffee, man, you bring the BEST coffee the world has ever seen." We live in a society where we want to jump the line and go straight to the top of organizations—or at least get paid like the leaders of our organizations. This is not reality. It takes time. However, if you are a salesperson selling tile flooring right now, be so undeniably good at what you do that you stand out from your peers. If you are selling pencils and erasers, be the best pencil and eraser salesperson that has ever existed. Success really is a mindset game, and it's our responsibility as salespeople to be great right where we are. Success will come. We all have to start from somewhere, so start with a winning attitude and be the best where you are at today. Or as Dabo goes on to say, "Bloom where you are planted."

Key Lesson:

The best Salespeople bring good to the culture they represent, are always a student of the game, and "bloom where they are planted."

Action Step:

Intentionally try to elevate your sales team this week. Send a Monday morning text message of encouragement, highlight a peer and the solid work they do, and/or praise instead of criticize. Watch the environment around you improve.

Thought to Consider:

Research by Manju Puri and David Robinson, business professors at Duke University, shows that optimistic people work harder, get paid more, are elected to office more often, and win at sports more regularly.

CHAPTER 14

THE POWER OF GOALS

"A goal is a dream with a deadline. Goals are the fuel in the furnace of achievement. If you don't know where you are going, you'll end up someplace else."
– John Maxwell

When I first had the opportunity to have a territory of my own, I kept hearing about this prestigious sales award that was nicknamed "The Eddie Award" after Eddie in New York who repeatedly won it. It was a very large check paid out to the Top Territory Manager who had the best two years in a row. "Yeah, it's a lot of money Jon, but don't worry, Eddie wins this award every year. You don't have a chance to win it—I mean he lives in New York City after all. He is way too talented and his territory is the biggest and the best," said one of my fellow teammates.

Initially, I took those comments in stride and didn't realize how much they bothered me. I just figured the game was rigged and aimed to just do my best with what I could control. But after a while, my competitive nature kicked in and it *really* started to bother me. Who is this Eddie guy after all? And why is he so much better than all of us? He's human, right? John Wooden termed the feeling I had stirring inside me as "Competitive Greatness." Well, this feeling started to kick in and it REALLY bothered me. I couldn't wrap my mind around how someone was this unbeatable.

After meeting Eddie at a National Meeting, I realized he *was* a great guy: smart, seasoned, and very professional. I could see why everyone feared him and saw him as the Michael Jordan or the LeBron James of our organization. But I *still* wanted to beat him, and I would not surrender my mind to defeat before I did everything in my power to compete and win.

I remained focused on my territory and for the first year, watched him from afar. That year he came in first, and I came in fourth out of 55 Territory Managers. In fact, the first two years prior to me working for this new company, Eddie came in first. He really had quite the streak going! During this time, I was reading a lot on goals and the importance of writing your goals down on paper. Author and leader John Maxwell's quote at the top of this chapter had a big impact on me. "Goals are the **fuel in the furnace of achievement**. If you don't know where you are going, you'll end up someplace else." Although at times I had my doubts, I did my best to control my internal dialogue. I wanted to be the best that I could be and was committed to giving it 100% of my ability.

Year Two came and sure enough, Eddie was leading through the first half of the year. The executives in our organization were singing his praises as he kicked off the year with a very large early win. I remained focused on writing my goals every week and looking at them each and every day. One of the first goals I had listed was "Become the 2016 Territory Manager of the Year on or before December 25th." Each month came and went and I kept inching up the score board. I developed the habit of spending about one to two hours midday on Saturdays planning out my next two weeks and writing and reviewing my goals. At one point mid-year it hit me … I can do this! Somebody has to win this award and why not me?!

Well, as the year went on and multiple Territory Managers were all in competition to win the esteemed "Eddie Award." I remember taking a walk with my wife one afternoon (she was pregnant with our first child, Ansley, and was due at the end of the year). We just walked and prayed, "God, we really want this award, we feel like we've put in the work, but you know our hearts. May your will be done."

Fast forward to the end. It stayed uncomfortably close as we all slugged it out, but by the grace of God I was able to come out on top. I was relieved and extremely grateful. Looking back, I realized you don't have to start with all the confidence in the world. It usually takes time to build.

Good habits, consistently performed over time, will compound, build momentum, and make you better at sales. James Clear, author of *Atomic Habits*, in his weekly newsletter, put it this way, "Asking what makes someone successful is like asking which ingredient makes a recipe taste good. It's not any single ingredient. It is the combination of many ingredients in the right proportions and in the right order—and the absence of anything that would ruin the mixture." Did writing my goals alone help me win this award? Probably not. However, writing my goals and trusting God were both part of the recipe that led to my success.

Key Lesson:

There is great power in writing your goals. Try writing goals that are S.M.A.R.T goals: Specific, Measurable, Attainable, Realistic, and Time-Bound.

A good example of this would be: "Become the number one sales representative and be honored with the Territory Manager of the Year Award on or before December 31st 20__." You fill in the blank!

Action Step:

Write your goals weekly and review them *every* day. You will subconsciously think about your goals and find ways to achieve them. I recommend three to five work goals per year. Put them on sticky notes all over your house and in your car.

Recording yourself stating your goals is also a powerful tool. Try videoing yourself when you feel at your best (sometimes after a great workout is the best time). Most people will hear this, think it's a little weird, and not take any action. For those brave enough to take action—you'll have a HUGE advantage.

Be sure to create some balance by creating goals outside of work (i.e. Spiritual, Personal, Financial, Family, and Fitness related). Download a free template at www.JonAlwinson.com.

Thought to Consider:

We all have equal opportunity to be great at sales. We all are born with unique gifts and talents. Believe in *your* God-given ability to be successful. You got this!

CHAPTER 15

SHOVEL THE ROCKS

Developing the Toughness
to Overcome Adversity

*"Show me someone who has done something worthwhile,
and I'll show you someone who has overcome adversity."*
– Lou Holtz

My wife is the consummate housekeeper and is always working to improve both the inside and outside of our home. Recently, I arrived home from a few days in the field working with my sales team and found my wife had ordered a pile of rocks that was now sitting in our driveway. *Four tons of rocks* to be exact! Being a product of public schools my whole life, I had to Google how much a ton weighed. A ton, for those of you like me who needed a reminder, is 2,000 pounds. I had *EIGHT THOUSAND POUNDS* of rocks I needed to move from my front driveway ALL the way to the edge of my back yard. I had two choices: I could complain and nothing would change except I would eventually get a letter telling me I was in violation of our HOA, *or* I could buckle my chin strap, keep my mouth shut, and get to work.

This mound of rocks seemed unconquerable. Quite honestly, there was a HUGE hill of painful work in front of me. As I made the countless trips back and forth from the front of my house to our backyard, it clicked. Shoveling rocks, as heavy, unpleasant, and painful as it was, represents what it's like being in sales. We put in countless hours of pre-call preparation, endure hard meetings when a prospect says "no," stay up late nights preparing and go on early morning drives, oftentimes hours on the road away from our families. All of this can be physically and mentally exhausting.

But stay the course! Stay strong, bite down on your mouth piece, and NEVER, EVER GIVE UP. It's times like these where it's critical to remember your why. Rewrite your goals and remain positive. It takes real toughness to endure the mental and physical challenge of tasks like these. By "shoveling the rocks," you are exercising your mental muscles at the same time as your physical muscles. That's why physical exercise is good training for sales! We need to push ourselves physically to develop and build the mental fortitude to be able to persist in the game of sales! I highly recommend you mix things up and start a new workout program if you've fallen off the wagon. I have a link on my webpage to a group that has phenomenal programs to help you build the physical and mental strength needed for success. Check out www.JonAlwinson.com for more.

Next, there's a very popular YouTube video in the personal development space from Jocko Willink called "Good." If you haven't watched this video, watch it at the end of this chapter. Jocko is an American hero. He's a famous former Navy Seal who not only has a decorated military career but has made a dramatic impact in the business world today. Jocko has also gained incredible popularity for posting a 4am picture of his watch on social media before a high intensity weight workout consistently for many years in a row. Hard work and grit is in his DNA.

In the video "Good," Jocko gets across the fact that when things are going wrong or going bad, our attitude should be that of "Good." "Didn't get promoted? GOOD, more time to get better." "Got beat? GOOD!" "Unexpected problems? GOOD! You have the opportunity to find a solution." Jocko ends the video imploring us to "Get Up, Reload, Re-Engage, and ATTACK." This video represents the relentless way. This is the mental strength we need every day and every week in the game of sales. If we don't toughen up, we too easily get broken down.

Sales doesn't have to be overly complicated. It does, however, require a large amount of mental fortitude—a Relentless spirit that will not be broken. If you are broken down right now or mentally fatigued, GOOD! It's an opportunity to fuel back up on books like this, remember your true identity, recalibrate your strategy, and as Jocko says, "attack" the game again. Sales isn't war, but it's often a tough environment. If you remain authentic, demonstrate that you truly care about your customers, develop your mental fortitude, and are willing to put in the work, you can and you will become successful.

One of the areas of discipline I've created over the years is Sunday night planning. It's a time where I update my emails, review and plan my calendar, and prepare a Monday morning message for my sales team. It's a time where I sacrifice Sunday Night Football and time with my family to prepare and stay ahead of the game. It's where I "shovel the rocks," and get my mind right for the week. Every time I want to quit, I think of my competition (both internal and external competition) and I dig a little deeper.

There are seasons in life where you will need to balance out your work and personal life (believe me, God and family are by *far* the most important). However, if you want to be great in sales, you must be obsessive about staying ahead of the game and constantly developing and improving. When you foster and develop a "shovel the rocks" mentality, you will separate yourself from the pack. It's usually through problems that opportunities are created and found. Are times difficult right now? Are things not easy? GOOD, opportunity is right around the corner!

Key Lesson:

Physical training is good for your sales game. How fit are you right now? And what are ways you can up your mental training too?

Action Step:

Start a consistent diet and physical training program today. Intentionally work on developing mental strength along the way. Go watch Jocko's YouTube video, "GOOD."

Thought to Consider:

On a scale of one to ten, how mentally tough are you right now? Write it down and do your best to move one level up over the next 90 days. No matter where you are on your journey, stay tough. Intentionally build in some type of consistent physical training. Don't quit, you can overcome! Oh, and go shovel some rocks and bring that mentality into your daily work.

CHAPTER 16

PREPARE NOW

It's Your Future We're Talking About!

*"Success is where **preparation** and opportunity meet."*
– Bobby Unser

There's a powerful story that highlights Dabo Swinney's incredible rise to leadership as the head football coach at Clemson University. This particular story does not directly focus on his elite leadership and winning attitude, although that is a powerful story in and of itself. Rather this story focuses on Dabo's legendary preparation that has made him one of the greatest coaches in sports history.

This story started years before Dabo ever took over as the interim head coach and subsequently as head coach of Clemson football, and is a key reason why Dabo received the head football coach position at all. You see, years before achieving this position, Dabo was **preparing *his* personal playbook** of everything he would do when he finally got his shot to become a head football coach one day. This playbook was chock-full of all the offensive and defensive plays his team would run. This playbook included special teams plays, red zone plays, and every aspect of football strategy. It even included the culture he expected out of his future team, both from the players and the coaches. Why is this important? If you take a step back and think about it, everything Dabo was doing years before he became head coach is *exactly* what you and I need to be doing as salespeople. It's elite preparation.

Have you heard of a successful way of dealing with people that you think might help you in your career? Write it down and put it in *your* book. Do you have goals for this coming sales year? Write it down and put it in *your* book. Have you heard a successful closing technique or series of questioning that you think can help you in your career? Write it down, practice, practice, and PRACTICE and put in *your* book.

You see, most people are not willing to "shovel the rocks" or are too lazy or fearful to take the effort to create their own Career Playbook. Life is too difficult, work is too hard, and as most people say, "I don't have the time." I would imagine Jocko Willink would respond, "GOOD" with a slight grin on his face. "*Good*, that means less competition for you, *good* that you are writing this down because that means more opportunities for you, *good* that you are prepared because most people are not prepared."

If you are reading this book and you've made it this far, you are built a little different. You want to win and are committing to a life that's different than others. Don't be afraid to be great! Commit to preparing like no other and separating yourself from the pack. Be like Dabo.

So how do you start preparing your personal playbook? Start today. The very first step in moving forward with your personal playbook is understanding where you want to go. This is often the most difficult as it can be tough to know exactly what you want to do with your career. If you are one of the fortunate ones, congratulations! If you need some more help, review Chapter 1 again and begin by reaching out to a mentor or potential mentor. Find someone trustworthy whose opinion you value and ask them for help.

Once you identify what you want to do, make up your mind to be a bulldog, to refuse to give up and go ALL IN with your efforts toward accomplishing that goal. Begin by either physically buying a notebook (three-ring binder, etc.) or electronically creating your notebook via a Microsoft Word document, PowerPoint, or Google Slides Presentation. I recommend doing this electronically as you can save, edit, and create a consistent playbook you can take with you throughout your career.

After understanding what your goal is (say it's becoming a Regional Sales Manager leading a team of 5-10 people), the second step is understanding how you are going to get there. Take inventory of your personal strengths. How is your current sales performance vs. others in similar roles? Are you a top performer and consistently hitting your sales goals? Are you taking stretch assignments in helping others or helping new hires understand sales? What are the areas of development that you need to improve, research, and implement to set you on your way? Become a student of your craft.

If you came over to my house, you would see an amount of physical sales books in my library that would make your jaw drop. Have I read every single book? No. But I've skimmed or read the majority. I want to know what every credible "expert" is saying about my craft so I can get where I want to go. Where are you currently on this journey? Are you studying your game and craft? In the example I gave above, if your goal is to become a sales leader, are you developing and studying leadership as much as you are sales? There are lots of questions in this chapter and a lot of good food for thought, I know. My hope is that this is leading you to the answers you want in your career.

Finally, after you've decided where you want to go and how you are going to get there, the last and arguably the most important step is taking massive action. Most sales jobs are not overly hard. The difficult part is dealing with people, and people are often inconsistent and unpredictable. When I say take massive action, I am referring to everything it takes to be successful. Three critical pillars for success are fueling up early in the morning with the right mindset, being willing to put in the work during the day, and putting in the after-hours effort.

We discussed earlier in this book about ensuring you are fueling up with positivity and time with God. Don't overlook this critical step. If you are not waking up early, you are setting yourself up for failure. You've heard it said time and time again that people buy from those whom they like and trust. Spending time with God each day creates a spirit of likeability in you like no other. Don't jump ahead here.

Albert Gray in *The Common Denominator of Success* says, "Every single qualification for success is acquired through habit. People form habits and habits form futures. If you do not deliberately form good habits, then unconsciously you will form bad ones. You are the kind of person you are because you have formed the habit of being that kind of person, and the only way you can change is through that habit." Spending time with God is the most important habit you can form and a HUGE competitive advantage.

Being willing to put in the work during the day is another important step in success. After you've identified the most critical areas where you need to spend your time, you must attack the game plan you've set for the week. Sometimes that means driving 2+ hours to an opportunity. Don't be the person who makes excuses and doesn't execute on the necessary steps needed for success. Simply put in the work with a smile on your face and a relentless spirit. This is where the rubber meets the road. So many salespeople want the reward of being great but are not willing to make the necessary sacrifices in their life to achieve this greatness. Don't let fear and hesitation derail you from your goals. Don't let the game of "ifs" become excuses for why you can't do something. Don't let excuses and fear cripple you from achieving what you want out of life.

Finally, consider what Jim Collins wrote in *Good to Great: Why Some Companies Make the Leap and Others Don't:* "Greatness is not a function of circumstance. Greatness, it turns out, is largely a matter of conscious choice, and discipline." The hour or two after dinner and before bedtime is a difference maker for *Relentless Sales* people. That time can be used for good or be wasted on mindless TV shows and the latest Netflix series. Consistently choosing to do a little extra during this time can set you up for success and give you an advantage over your peers and competition. It's your choice. Fire off a few extra emails, re-write and reorganize your *Weekly Attack List* (Chapter 7), pre-call plan, or waste it "recharging" watching wasteful television. Success really is a choice, so choose wisely!

Key Lesson:

- The first step is understanding where you want to go.
- The second step is identifying how you are going to get there.
- The third step is taking massive action.

Action Step:

Start creating your personal playbook today. Save this on your computer and print the pages out as you create them. Have both a hard copy and a saved copy on your computer.

Thought to Consider:

"Spectacular achievement is always preceded by unspectacular preparation." – Robert H. Schuller

CHAPTER 17

REDEFINING FAILURE

"Success consists of going from failure to failure without loss of enthusiasm."
– Winston Churchill

I'm finally starting to embrace and understand failure a little more. When I was as kid, I never wanted to make any mistakes. I HATED messing up at anything. As a parent, I'm starting to wake up to the incredible benefits of failure. My sweet Ansley is seven years old and I am constantly asking her, "What's one thing you failed at today?" She always tells me nothing, but I'm persistent with my questioning. I want her to know that failure is OK in our house and is proof we are trying hard things and pursing greatness. If you have no failure in your life, you probably don't have big enough goals or are not trying to accomplish difficult things.

When it comes to sales, failure is tricky, because it affects the bottom line and your sales rankings. So how do we deal with failure? Justin, who I referenced in Chapter 4, would always coach us to "let the bat off our shoulders" and "swing for the fences." We shouldn't be reckless, but if we've put in the work and demonstrated great value to our customers, we have to go for it. This is especially important when you are utterly convinced your product, service, or solution is the best quality, value, and option for your customers.

I've also found that when you have a full pipeline of opportunities, it gives you more confidence that the deal you are currently working on isn't "all or nothing" and it isn't the end of the world if you win the deal or not. Action significantly helps to reduce fears when it comes to sales. There's an attractive confidence that arises when you don't come off as desperate and needy. A solid pipeline is your lifeblood, and when you combine it with action you become a force to be reckoned with.

I've failed so many times in my sales career that it's hard for me to recall all my mistakes along the way. To ensure that I'm learning from my mistakes and not just forgetting about them, I've created a system to help me process my failures and harness them for my personal growth. I created folders in the Notes app on my phone that's called "Things I Am Learning" for the particular year I am in. This helps me keep track of the lessons I've learned along the way, and reviewing them regularly is a helpful step in my personal development plan.

A piece of advice I received years ago was to remember the lessons and forget the details. Or, as my friend Stephen likes to say, "Eat the chicken and spit out the bones." I love that! So, when I make a mistake, particularly a tactical error, I write it down in my phone app and put the specific lesson I learned from my mistake. I try not to write an essay, but rather the important details that can help me not repeat that mistake in the future.

I'm also a believer that real-time coaching can help us reduce our failures. There's a vivid memory I have of working with a hospital system in South Georgia on a very large capital sales opportunity. I had a very good strategy and worked my sales process to the best of my ability. I had strong physician support, excellent relationships, good interaction and communication with the materials management team, and the clinical nursing team were "for me" and for the opportunity I had presented to the hospital system. I had properly evaluated the technology I was proposing and had "put in the work" necessary to win the deal.

Yet there was one stakeholder that I was missing. I knew it, and my manager knew it. As I was preparing to hit reverse in my car and head back north to Atlanta, he said, "Jon, don't be a _____ and get your 'you-know-what' back in there, and don't leave until you speak to that person." He was right, and I knew it.

At first, I was angry, but I sucked up my pride and did exactly as he told me. It worked! I brought a negative person over to being neutral or even slightly positive about the opportunity. What's funny is not only did I get the deal I was working on, but I was able to get an identical deal later that year that pushed me over the top for the number one salesperson for my company that year. Had I not listened to my manager and chickened out so as not to risk failure, who knows where I would be today? It just goes to show you how important it is to be coachable and willing to go the extra mile. If you're interested in free coaching resources, check out www.JonAlwinson.com for more information.

Finally, failure is not the boogeyman. We learn so much about ourselves when we are willing to put it all on the line and go for it. We learn what works and subsequently what doesn't work along the way. But we must be willing to risk our pride and risk our livelihoods when we are in sales. It's part of the job. John Maxwell in his timeless book Fail Forward put it this way, "The essence of man is imperfection. Know that you're going to make mistakes. The fellow who never makes a mistake takes his orders from one who does. Wake up and realize this: Failure is simply a price we pay to achieve success."

Maxwell goes on to say, "Embrace adversity and make failure a regular part of your life. If you're not failing, you're probably not really moving forward." Don't be afraid to fail.

Everything in life brings risk. It's true that you risk failure if you try something bold because you might miss it. But you also risk failure if you stand still and don't try anything new. Let the bat off your shoulder and swing for the fences!

Key Lesson:

Failure often precedes success. If we change our perspective on failure, it sets us up for a lifetime of success.

Action Step:

Create a "Things I Am Learning" note in your phone today. Write down the things that make you wince and refer back to them regularly. Remember the lessons and forget the details.

Thought to Consider:

"Through our pain and disappointments come a sense of great purpose, a greater commitment to our craft, and a relentless pursuit of our dreams. Without going through this process, we cannot truly find the excellence we have from within."
– The Daily Coach, December 19th, 2022

CHAPTER 18

BE YOU

*"A good name is to be chosen rather than great riches,
and favor is better than silver and gold."*
- Proverbs 22:1

We care too much about what other people think of us, don't we? Especially us salespeople. We work in the "people business" and developing relationships and getting people to like us become part of our DNA. Think about how deeply we hyper-analyze our interactions and armchair quarterback our recent sales calls. Part of our job is to get others to like us, but often that causes us to be constantly inundated with trying to be "on" at all times. Relax. Don't put so much pressure on yourself. When you can step back, think clearly, and realize that God has you *exactly* where he wants you for a reason, it puts life into proper perspective and frees you up to take care of your customers and to sell authentically.

I remember back in 2019 when I had a territory realignment and picked up a new territory manager in New Orleans named Jack. Jack is truly a one-of-a-kind personality and has become a close friend over the years. When Jack joined my team, I quickly realized he was extremely funny, but was very nervous initially when he was in-person with his customers. When he was with me and our sales team, he was self-deprecating, goofy, and absolutely hilarious. But when he was in front of his customers, he became quieter than usual and he was very uncomfortable.

I remember walking out of a meeting, looking directly at him, and saying, "You need to start having fun and being yourself with your customers. You don't realize it, but you are trying to be this overly buttoned-up sales persona and that's not you. Just smile, be inquisitive, be funny, and be yourself. Just be Jack!"

"But what if the customers have a clinical question that I don't know?" Jack was clearly overthinking it. He was falling into the trap of the 'what ifs.'

"Forget the what ifs," I said. "If you don't know the answer, then you simply tell them you don't know and you will look into it and get back to them as quickly as possible. What I *need* you to do is start smiling immediately, and just be YOU. You are making your customers uncomfortable by not being yourself. You are a really funny and smart guy, let them see your true personality."

After some time, Jack did just that. He started working on being his authentic, "fun Jack" self with his customers. The results? Jack's numbers took off like a rocket over the next twelve months and he went from being at the bottom of the sales board to top ten by the end of the year. Was it a fluke? Not at all.

During one of my next field rides with Jack, he literally had the CEO of a large account belly laughing at his jokes as we sat in her office before she signed a long-term partnership deal with our organization. Jack was hitting his stride, his confidence was at an all-time high, and it was so much fun to watch. Later he told me, "I thought I missed my calling as a game show host, but *this job* will suffice for the time being."

As hilarious as that is, the lesson is to live authentically. Not only is it way more fun, but your impact will be so much greater if you just be yourself.

Jamie, one of my closest mentors, always reminds me of the famous Teddy Roosevelt quote: "People (your customers) don't care how much you know, until they know how much you care." Don't worry about having all the answers. Yes, prepare and do your best to be excellent. But have FUN, smile, and truly care about your customers. When you do this consistently, you set yourself up for a career chock-full of success in sales.

John Mason, author of *An Enemy Called Average*, put it this way: "The call in your life is not a copy. In this day of peer pressure, trends, and fads, we need to realize and accept that each person has been custom-made by God the Creator. Each of us has a unique and personal call upon our lives. We are to be our own selves and not a copy of others."

Remember from Chapter 2 that you should live *from* your identity, not *for* your identity. When you do that, it frees you up to smile big and truly listen to your customers so you can match your service and product offerings up for what *they* truly care about.

For the last 15+ years, I've reflected on these principles and lessons and my hope is that you can pull wisdom from each of the chapters in this book to help you develop the skills, mentality, and faith needed to be great at sales.

You know, I must admit, my journey is just beginning. I'm like a white belt in jujitsu who just received his first stripe. I can recognize that in the path in front of me, I still have so much to learn. I know this because I've been a witness to many great people ahead of me in this journey, who I hope to continue learning from. For each of us, the journey of developing our character, mentality, and skills as salespeople will continue on for a long, long time.

My hope for you is that no matter where you are on your journey, you can glean value from what you've read in this book and stay relentless as you strive to become a little better each day. But most importantly, that you can use the tools and skills described in this book to positively impact and encourage the lives of others around you. I'd love to keep in touch. Connect with me on social media and let's keep pushing each other to greatness!

Key Lesson:

Be your authentic self.

Action Step:

Connect with me on social media or email me at Jon@AlwinsonBooks.com.

Join our text thread each week for motivation!
Text me directly at 404-272-5236 to join up.

Thought to Consider:

"Our preference for instant gratification reveals an important truth about success: because of how we are wired, most people will spend all day chasing quick hits of satisfaction. The road less traveled is the road of delayed gratification. If you're willing to wait for the rewards, you'll face less competition and often get a bigger payoff. As the saying goes, the last mile is always the least crowded." – James Clear, Chapter 15 of *Atomic Habits*

ABOUT THE AUTHOR

Jon Alwinson lives in Atlanta, GA, with his wife, Sandra, and two children, Ansley and Easton. Jon loves spending time with his family and doing anything outdoors, including fishing, hunting, and sports of all kinds. He and his family attend Passion City Church and want everyone to maximize their professional careers and find hope in Jesus.

If you enjoyed this book, please considering leaving a review online, as it helps others discover it. Make sure to visit **www.JonAlwinson.com** to find the various resources listed in this book and to join our monthly newsletter. Send Jon a text at 404-272-5236 to participate in his weekly motivational text thread. Additionally, connect with Jon on LinkedIn, Instagram, Facebook, or on X (formally known as Twitter).

Made in United States
Orlando, FL
12 December 2023

40840050R00091